COPYRIGHT

First published - August 2013.

Revised edition - March 2017.

BOOK REVIEW

Mysteries of Kenya is a great read, a wonderful combination of the author's personal anecdotes, fascinating facts about Kenya, and background history about the country. The author's knowledge and affection for his homeland is clearly transmitted as he leads the reader on a tour of the key areas, and his own photographs which illustrate the book are truly wonderful.

I very much enjoyed reading this book and looking at the photographs, both of which have given me a new respect for Kenya and its people. My knowledge which was woefully lacking has been much improved, and the author's gentle enthusiasm can't help but be transmitted to the reader.

I recommend this book as an excellent read.

Louise Chick, St Albans

H. E. Mr Ephraim W. Ngare
High Commissioner

KENYA HIGH COMMISSION
45 Portland Place, London W1B 1AS, United Kingdom

Tel: 020-7636 2371 Fax: 020-7323 6717
E-mail: kcomm45@aol.com

16th July, 2013

Mysteries of Kenya Revealed gives a vivid and fascinating insight into the many treasures – cultural, historical, physical, environmental, wildlife and more – that Kenya has to offer its visitors and inhabitants. Its author Mr Harish Luther, a Kenya Citizen with deep affection and respect for Kenya, has an impressive knowledge and understanding of his country and these qualities are pivotal in making the journey through Kenya so spectacular and inspiring! With an engaging narrative, combining humour with fact, plus personal insight accompanied by an incredible collection of stunning photographs all taken by the author and showcasing Kenya in its many colours. The reader is guaranteed a fantastic opportunity to explore a very beautiful and unique country.

A very informative book and I would highly recommend it.

Ephraim W. Ngare
High Commissioner
Kenya High Commission, London

Contents

Preface

About the Author

I am Harish Luther. I was born, educated and married in Kenya and am a Kenyan citizen of Indian origin. My great-grandfather came to Kenya in the early 1910s followed by my grandfather in 1917. My father was born there in 1922 and I was born in 1948. All three of my children were also born there.

I started my passion for photography at a very early age when my father bought me my first camera, a Kodak Brownie. Then in 1965 he bought me a Minolta SRT 303 camera, which gave me the incentive to develop my knowledge of photography even further. Having used the Minolta camera for five years I then bought my first Nikon camera—the Nikkormat FTN—and since then I have pledged my allegiance to Nikon cameras. With the advent of digital photography I very reluctantly moved from film to digital cameras, and now I only use the latest Nikon Digital Professional cameras and lenses.

While in Kenya, I worked as a Hospital and Surgical Supplies Representative, covering the whole of the country. I always took my camera along with me which made it easier for me to take photographs all over Kenya. I travelled extensively in my job and have been to all the popular National Parks. This travelling gave me a very unique insight into and knowledge of Kenya.

During my many travels I have been chased by rhinos, buffalos and elephants and have made eye-to-eye contact with the big cats. I have fortunately lived to tell the tale, as I have always given the animals all the space and respect that they needed.

Currently I am living in England, with my children and four lovely granddaughters. I give lectures about Kenya to clubs, schools, institutions and camera clubs and regularly return to my roots in Kenya to update my photographs.

Another of my passions is mountain climbing and trekking, which I started whilst I was living in Kenya. Nowadays I share this passion through leading climbing and trekking trips to both Mount Kilimanjaro and Mount Kenya. After climbing Mount Kilimanjaro I then lead clients on wildlife safaris in Tanzania, either to Lake Manyara National Park or Tarangire National Park, depending on the time of year. Thereafter we go to the Olduvai Gorge, Serengeti National Park and lastly the Ngorongoro Crater.

The wildlife safaris in Kenya involve the most popular Game Reserves and National Parks, e.g. Masai Mara Game Reserve, Samburu Game Reserve, Aberdare National Park, Lake Nakuru National Park, Amboseli National Park and Nairobi National Park.

I always wanted to share my life experiences and photographs with the rest of the world, and this book is my invitation to you to see Kenya through my eyes and memories. I sincerely hope that you will enjoy the many sights and colours of Kenya as much as I have enjoyed the process of compiling and recording them.

Dedication

I would like to dedicate this book to the memory of my late father, who unknowingly set me on the path to becoming a photographer in my later life. I am what I am today because of all the help that he gave me when I was growing up, and for that I thank him.

I would also like to dedicate it to my four lovely granddaughters, Naina, Anisha, Isha and Lana, who give me complete joy in my life. I hope that I can teach and guide them in their lives, and maybe one of them will follow in my footsteps or as we say in Kenya, 'Fata Nyayo' (which means 'follow in my footsteps').

This book is also dedicated to my wife Parvinder and my children, Poonam, Sunita and Amandeep for being with me and roughing it out with me during my photographic travels.

Acknowledgements

I am indebted to the following people for their help and support:

My brother Rajeshwar, who gave me his wildebeest migration photos.

My cousin Mrs Madhu Walia and my friends Rajinder Singh Shukla and Manmohan Aggarwal, for encouraging me to write this book and also reading the first draft. Rajinder Shukla also helped in colour correcting some of the photos.

My sister Shashi and brother-in-law Harmesh Mangrah, for checking the book and making some suggestions.

My work colleague Lin Phillips, for correcting punctuation for me and constantly encouraging me to write the book.

Mrs Irene Lakhani for proof reading the book and doing corrections where needed.

Colourprint Kenya Ltd. for design, typeset and layout of the book.

Mr Dean Cunningham for designing the cover.

Mr Mohammed Shoaib Graphic Designer and editor.

Kenya's Big Five

1. History

Kenya around the 1890s was a vast uninhabited, dry, desolate, wild, and malaria-infested country. The British had taken over both Kenya and Uganda. Dr. David Livingstone had already 'discovered' the source of the River Nile. The British government had built an ox-cart track from the Kenyan town of Mombasa, which had a sea port, to Busia on the border between Kenya and the landlocked Uganda - a distance of about 660 miles. Then in 1896 the government decided to build a railway line from Mombasa to the Ugandan capital, Kampala.

In order to build this railway line—which would link Uganda to the coast—all kinds of workers were needed. The management team came from England, while the artisans and labourers came from India, which was then a colony of the British Empire. This railway line was called the Kenya Uganda Railways (KUR) – also known as 'the Lunatic Express'; this is very well documented in other media, so I will not spend time on it here. The route of the KUR line was from Mombasa to Nairobi through the Tsavo National Park (known for the Man-Eaters of Tsavo). From Nairobi the track went through the Rift Valley via Limuru, Naivasha, Nakuru, Timboroa, Eldoret and Bungoma. Timboroa is Kenya's highest train station, at an elevation of about 9000 feet, and it's also the world's highest train station on the equator. From Bungoma, the railway track passed into Uganda via Tororo and then on to Kampala.

A bridge that was built in 1927 to support a stretch of the railway line on its journey inland between the Mombasa Port and Uganda is still standing and in use in Mombasa. The KUR logo and the year it was completed, is clearly visible on its side.

After the railway line was completed, the artisans and labourers decided to stay behind in Kenya rather than go back to India. They eventually started bringing their families to Kenya. This growing population had its own requirements, such as housing, hospitals, schools for its children and Indian food. Also within the population were the shopkeepers and schoolteachers. Amongst these teachers was my grandfather, Master Amarnath, who taught mathematics up to 'O' level at the then Government Indian High School in Nairobi. This school's name was later changed to 'The Duke of Gloucester High School' and nowadays it is called 'The Jamhuri High School'. My grandfather was in fact the teacher responsible for setting the Cambridge University mathematics 'O' Level exams for the whole of East Africa.

The British government started building the infrastructure required to house the growing population of its colony, including roads, houses, shops, hospitals and schools.

This growing population eventually started to go into business. The White British started acquiring land and became big farm owners as they acquired the best lands in the best areas of Kenya. This later became known as the White Highlands. The Indians were prevented from owning any land in the White Highlands and hence started opening their own shops and other small businesses. These Indian shopkeepers saw a business opportunity and moved from the main towns into the country villages, so every local village in the country had at least one Indian shopkeeper, who was able to supply 'anything' that anybody wanted. If he did not have an item in store he knew where to get it from, even if not immediately, and would be able to deliver it to the customer. These Indian shopkeepers were known locally as DUKAWALLAS. These dukawallas were able to supply all the needs of the Indians, the local Africans and the White farmers.

Kenya's two neighbouring countries, Uganda and Tanganyika, were also colonies of the British Empire; these three countries were collectively known as 'The Colonies and Protectorate of the British Empire'. Up to the 1920s Northern Tanganyika was ruled by Germany, which is why there is still a strong German legacy of in Northern Tanganyika, e.g. the first person to climb Mount Kilimanjaro was a German, Hans Meyer in 1889.

HANS MEYER,
THE FIRST EUROPEAN EXPLORER WHO
CONQUERED THE SUMMIT OF MOUNT
KILIMANJARO IN 1889.

The plaque commemorating Hans Meyer at the start of the Marangu route on Mount Kilimanjaro, in Tanzania

Southern Tanganyika was ruled by the British. During the First World War, some fighting took place here, and the Germans eventually lost. The whole of Tanganyika then became a colony of the British Empire. Tanganyika achieved its independence from Britain on 9th December 1961, Uganda on 9th October 1962 and Kenya on 12th December 1963.

Tanganyika's neighbour in the east is a small island called Zanzibar. It was ruled by a Sultan, hence it was also called 'The Sultanate of Zanzibar'. However, in 1964 some mercenaries under the command of Field Marshall John Okello came and overthrew the Sultan. Tanganyika and Zanzibar then amalgamated to form one big country which is now called Tanzania. The word **Tanzania** is a derivative of '**Tan**ganyika **Zan**zibar **I**ndependent **A**ssociation'.

While the British were ruling Kenya they acquired the best lands for themselves, but at the same time they also built the infrastructure of the country, i.e. they built all the major roads, shops, houses and the airport. Kenya's first airport was located in the Eastleigh area of Nairobi. After Kenya's independence this became the base and headquarters of the Kenya Air Force. Thereafter, Kenya built a civilian airport at Embakasi to handle all the big aeroplanes andthis was called the Embakasi Airport. Its name was later changed to the Jomo Kenyatta International Airport (JKIA), so named after Kenya's first President, Mzee Jomo Kenyatta.

In all the towns of Kenya, the White British segregated the population according to the colour of their skin. They gave themselves the best areas of every town while the Africans were housed in the slums and all the Asians were in the remaining areas. The British did not know the difference between the various Asians, i.e. the Hindu Punjabis, the Hindu Gujaratis (Shahs, Patels, Lohanas), the Muslims (Shias, Sunnis, Ismailis), and the Goans, so they were all housed in one area. For the Asians this meant that we all became aware of each other's languages and cultures, and this resulted, thanks to the British, in the Asians from East Africa now being multilingual and able to speak 5 or 6 languages, e.g. English, Swahili (the national language of East Africa), Hindi, Punjabi, Urdu and Gujarati. Thus, Kenya is one of the few countries in the world where all the various religious and multi-ethnic communities live together in complete harmony.

The following information is from Wikipedia

There is another, perhaps less expected, 'face' of Kenya. Being a country of very warm temperatures throughout the year, it has had an attachment with Hollywood that dates back to the 1930s. Many classic adventure films were shot on location in Kenya, including *The Snows of Kilimanjaro* starring Gregory Peck, *King Solomon's Mines* with Stewart Granger, *Mogambo* featuring Clark Gable and Ava Gardner, and *The African Queen* starring Humphrey Bogart and Katherine Hepburn. The film *Hatari*, starring John Wayne and Hardy Kruger, was filmed in Tanzania.

The two latest Hollywood films shot in Kenya are "Born Free" starring Bill Travers and Virginia McKenna and also "Out of Africa" starring Robert Redford and Meryl Streep.

2. Culture & General Information

Kenya is located on the eastern side of Africa, with the equator dividing the country into two almost equal halves. It is surrounded by the Indian Ocean on its east and it is bordered by five countries: Somalia in the north-east, Ethiopia in the north, South Sudan in the north-west, Uganda in the west and Tanzania in the south. Kenya has two inland bodies of water; Lake Turkana in the north and Lake Victoria in the west. Lake Victoria is the world's second largest fresh water Lake (after Lake Superior in the US and Canada) and the world's largest tropical lake. It is shared by Uganda and Tanzania, with the bulk of it being in Tanzania.

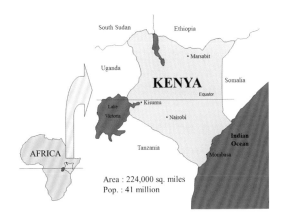

Kenya—a medium-sized country by continental standards—is named after Mount Kenya, which is Africa's second highest mountain. It covers an area of about 586,600 square kilometrs or 224,000 square miles and has a population of about 41 million people, representing 42 different tribes and cultures. Some 60% of this population is under the age of 15. The annual population growth rate is 4%, which is nearly the highest in the world.

- Population 41 million
- 60% under the age of 15
- 4% annual growth rate

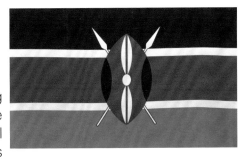

Kenya has three major cities: **Nairobi**, being the capital, is situated in the center of the country and is the regional and commercial hub; **Mombasa** is the port city and is surrounded by the Indian Ocean; **Kisumu,** located on Lake Victoria, is the centre for the Fisheries Department because of the abundant amount of fish found in the lake. The other towns of importance are Nyeri, which is at the base of Mount Kenya, and then Eldoret and Kitale which are in the Highlands area.

Kenya has four international airports; Jomo Kenyatta International Airport in Nairobi, Mombasa International Airport, Kisumu International Airport and Eldoret International Airport. The Nairobi and Mombasa airports are the entry points for most of the tourists who come to visit Kenya and since 31st December 2010 Kenya recorded the highest number of tourist arrivals ever, at over one million visitors.

The equator divides Kenya roughly into two halves. The top half is semi-arid with near-desert landscapes; this area borders with Somalia, Ethiopia and South Sudan. The lower half is where most of the population lives. This is also because Kenya has two major rivers which start in the Highlands and travel in an easterly direction to the coast. The Tana River starts from the Mount Kenya region while the Athi River starts from the Aberdare Mountain range. Two other rivers, Mara and Migori, start in the Mua Hills and travel in a westerly direction towards Lake Victoria. Since water is essential for living, this is where the majority of the population is found.

The eastern wall of the Great Rift Valley bisects Kenya from north to south, thereby creating different geographical and climatic zones. There is the warmer climate all along the coast. Then as you move inland towards Nairobi the geography changes to wildlife-rich savannah grasslands. Nairobi, at an altitude of 5500 feet has a cool climate. This climate then gets colder as you move towards Mount Kenya, which has three permanently snow-capped peaks – Batian, Nelion and Point Lenana. All the White Highlands are in the Rift Valley which is a very fertile land. Most of the food for Kenya's population is grown in the Highlands area.

Once past the Highlands, the warm and humid tropical climate re-appears further inland towards Lake Victoria, before again giving way to temperate forested and hilly areas in the western region.

Kenya is basically an agricultural country. Agriculture is a major employer and the country traditionally exports tea and coffee, and more recently fresh flowers to Europe. The Kenyan government realized early on the importance of its natural resources i.e. its wildlife, and so took steps to encourage and nurture tourism. Now Kenya's biggest foreign exchange earnings come from tourism. The following bar chart shows the contributions from various sectors in Kenya Shillings (in billions).

Contributions by Sectors – KShs Billion
(KShs 130.00 = £1   KShs 1M = £7,692)

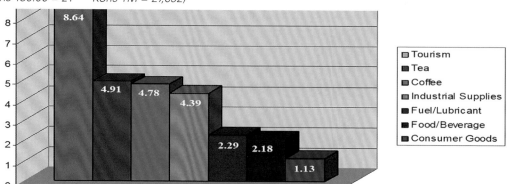

Kenya is famous for its wildlife safaris and diverse world-famous wildlife reserves and National Parks such as the Masai Mara Game Reserve, Samburu Game Reserve, Tsavo National Park, Lake Nakuru National Park, Aberdare National Park, Amboseli National Park and Mount Kenya National Park attract tourists from all over the world. Nairobi National Park is situated right next to Nairobi, Kenya's capital city. This is unique, as this is the only place in the world where there is a National Park right next to a capital city.

With all of these diverse activities on offer, Kenya can be described as a land of:

- **wildlife**
- **sunshine**
- **white sandy beaches**
- **snow and ice on the equator**
- **beautiful sunrises and sunsets.**

The following photographs demonstrate Kenya's impressive offering:

Kenya - a land of wildlife

Kenya - a land of white sandy beaches

Kenya - a land of sunshine

Kenya - a land of snow and ice on the equator. The only country in the world on the equator to have permanent snow and ice throughout the year.

Kenya - a land of beautiful sunrises and sunsets

After tourism, the next biggest foreign exchange earner for Kenya is agriculture, which comprises tea, coffee and flowers, e.g. roses, orchids and carnations.

Tea

Coffee

Flowers - roses, orchids and carnations

It was reported in the British press that for the funeral of Diana, Princess of Wales, in August 1997, nearly 90% of the flowers and bouquets came from Kenya!

In the late 1930s an English writer, Elspeth Huxley, travelled from Nairobi to Thika, a distance of about 30 miles. Nearing Thika, she saw some trees which looked as though they were on fire. As she came closer, she saw that the trees were not actually on fire but that they had on them bright red flowers which, en masse, resembled a fire and so she aptly named the trees 'Nandi Flame Trees' with 'Nandi Flames flowers'. Afterwards, Elspeth Huxley wrote a book entitled *The Flame Trees of Thika*.

Being in the tropics, Kenya is blessed with an abundance of sunshine which produces a variety of colourful flowers of various shapes and sizes.

In the Western world there is no problem with obtaining gas for cooking and heating purposes as it's supplied in underground pipes. In Kenya, however, the majority of the population lives outside the main towns, so instead of gas they have to use firewood. This is collected and brought home by the women. These women sometimes have to walk long distances and even go into the forests just to collect wood. The forests can sometimes be a few miles away from the village. So the women trek to the forest and chop down a few trees for their needs. But in the forests there is also the danger of being attacked by wild animals such as buffalos and elephants. For this reason the women go to the forests in small groups and they stay close to each other. This gives group protection to everyone.

This mud-walled hut with a thatched roof is very typical of the Kikuyu tribe. You can see the firewood that has been collected earlier by the women stacked just outside the hut. During the cold weather the women keep the fires lit inside the huts to keep them warm. Interestingly though, people do not die from carbon monoxide poisoning because the thatched roof is so well constructed and very well ventilated that all the poisonous gases escape up and out of the huts.

Below is a typical Masai hut called a Masai Manyatta

In addition to and in contrast with the mud-walled huts in the rural areas of Kenya, there are ultra-modern buildings in the urban areas. At the moment Kenya is enjoying prosperity with a property boom: everywhere you go in any of the major towns of Kenya, you will see lots of new multi-storey buildings, either completed or under construction. New buildings in any location always signify prosperity and so it is with Kenya.

With the construction of all these new buildings, the population of the urban areas just keeps increasing and this in turn increases the quantities of garbage produced in the towns. In this respect the Kenyans are very industrious: they sift through the garbage and collect all the recyclable materials, e.g. plastic bottles, plastic sheets, newspapers, magazines and plastic bags. These are then sold to recycling companies for profit. This enables those individuals who sell the materials to earn some money to sustain themselves and their families.

Plastic bottles

Plastic sheets

Because of Kenya's proximity to the equator there are occasionally water shortages in the towns during the two dry seasons. To solve this problem, some people earn their living by supplying water to the residents in plastic containers, transporting and distributing them around town by handcarts.

3. Transport

As a country, Kenya has developed because of its fundamental need for transport. The railway line from Mombasa to Kampala, for example, was constructed in order to make accessible the landlocked Uganda. If you look at any maps of Kenya, you will see that the general population lives in close proximity to the railway tracks or rail transport links and this applies to the all major roads in the country as well.

When the railway line reached Nairobi, the halfway point between Mombasa and Kampala, the construction team halted work here and made Nairobi their head quarters. All the required infrastructure was then built around Nairobi e.g. Nairobi railway station, the City Hall, the law courts, parliament buildings, government house, hospitals, shops, schools, tarmac roads, sewage and water supplies.

Nairobi Railway Station, front view

An interesting fact about Nairobi's railway station is that the building which stands today is the original one in its entirety. In fact, the director of the film *Out of Africa,* starring Robert Redford and Meryl Streep, is on record as saying that, for their shooting scenes involving the station, they did not have to use any props, as everything there was in its original, authentic form. So the Nairobi Railway Station is a fully functional listed and historical building.

This is how the Nairobi Railway Station looks from across the footbridge at the station. But with the modernisation of the station this view will change in a few years' time.

At the Nairobi Railway Museum there are three very important items which we all can relate to.

The first one is the special seat which was used by President Roosevelt of the United States during his hunting trip to Kenya. This seat was fixed to the front of an engine thereby giving President Roosevelt a clear shot at whatever he was hunting.

Here I am sitting in the same seat with the engine shape printed behind on the wall.

Then there is the arm chair which was used by Queen Elizabeth II during her visit to Kenya in the early 1950s.

And lastly there is the train which was used during the filming of the movie 'Out of Africa'.

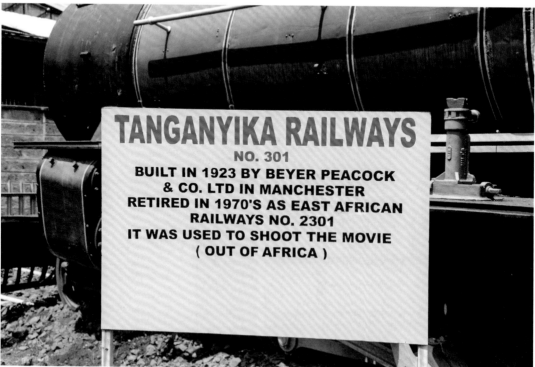

This plaque is placed next to the engine

When this railway line was built only steam locomotives were used and the track was a narrow-gauge one. These steam locomotives are no longer in service but are kept in the Nairobi Railway Museum. Occasionally they are taken out for commemorative rides between Nairobi and Naivasha in the Rift Valley, a distance of about 50 miles. The steam locomotives have now been replaced with diesel locomotives, but still on a narrow-gauge track.

A steam locomotive being filled with water and a diesel locomotive on the right

If you compare these three photographs of the three engines, you will see that the steam engine is very bulky as it has to carry a lot of water in order to generate the steam to drive the engine. It has to constantly keep on refilling its tanks with water. The diesel engine is smaller than the steam engine as it carries all its diesel on board and does not have to refuel on the way. The electric train is the smallest in size, is streamlined and gets its power from the overhead electric cables.

An electric train in England

In Kenya to this day they are still using narrow-gauge railway tracks, while in the Western world they have moved onto wide-gauge tracks. The physical difference between the two gauges is clearly evident in the two photos below.

Narrow gauge track in Kenya   Wide gauge track in England

The steam and diesel locomotives can only be used on the narrow-gauge track, while the faster electric trains can only be used on the wide-gauge track. To put this in perspective: to travel from Nairobi to Mombasa—a distance of 300 miles—on a narrow-gauge track would take about 12 hours while on a wide-gauge track only 3 hours!

The Kenya Government has put into place some very ambitious programmes to upgrade the Railway infrastructure in the next ten years. Firstly the whole of the Kenya Railways tracks are to be changed to the wide-gauge tracks so that the time taken to travel to Mombasa can be reduced from the present 12 hours to just 3 hours.

The town of Lamu on Kenya's northern coast is to be upgraded into a port. It will have a railway station and also a domestic airport. A tarmac road and a railway line will be built linking Lamu to Isiolo in northern Kenya. Isiolo is a small town about 200 miles north of Nairobi, Kenya's capital. From Isiolo the railway line and the tarmac road will continue towards South Sudan and Ethiopia. This is because the oil that has been discovered in northern Kenya and also to open up South Sudan and Ethiopia which are both land locked countries. Isiolo will then become the hub of all these activities.

Timboroa Railway Station needs mentioning because it is the world's highest railway station on the equator at an altitude of 2743 meters or 9001 feet and is on the main railway line from Nairobi in Kenya to Kampala in Uganda.

This is the view of the Timboroa Railway Station with a train on the siding and the Station Master's building on the right.

This Station Master's building is the original building which was built at the same time as the railway line. In fact nearly all of the railway stations that were built then were built in exactly the same way. In this building you could purchase your tickets for your journey.

The Timboroa Railway Station Masters building

In this building all of the equipment is still in use even though it is already antique e.g. the old Morse code machine, the keys for directing the railway onto specific tracks and also the wooden ring with a key which the train driver has to carry with him. On a single-track line, as long as the train driver has this ring with him, he knows that the next section of the line in front is clear. So he can travel without fear of an accident with a train approaching from the opposite direction.

Here the Station Master is holding the wooden ring with the leather pouch which contains the key for the clear passage.

In most parts of the world, the rails are moved from one track to another by electrical means. But here in Timboroa and in fact in most of Kenya's railway stations, the tracks are changed manually using a steel wire and manual levers as shown here.

Kenya's old and antique railway system needs to be upgraded and this is being undertaken by the Kenya Government with help from the Chinese Government. So very soon Kenya will have a modern railway system and all of these antique items will be put into the Railway Museum so that future generations will know how we all used to travel.

Despite Kenya being such a modern country with many tarmacked roads, its transport infrastructure is not very highly developed in the rural areas. But the roads in Nairobi are being upgraded. At the moment a six lane Nairobi - Thika Super Highway has being built a distance of about 30 miles. Hence Thika has now become a suburb of Nairobi.

Nairobi to Thika road around the Kenya Breweries.

To ease the traffic congestion in Nairobi flyovers have being built at the busy intersections at the Museum Hill roundabout, the Globe Cinema roundabout and in Pangani at the Forest Road and Muranga Road junctions.

Museum Hill flyover

Globe Cinema roundabout flyover.

Pangani flyover

Pedesterian foot bridge near Pangani flyover.

There is also a plan to build an elevated road from the Westlands area of Nairobi to the JKIA at Embakasi.

In the rural areas the people here use their own vehicles or 'pick-ups' as a means of transporting people and goods. These local 'pick-ups', or illegal taxis, are commonly known as 'MATATUS'. These Matatus will stop and go wherever there are people, as people equal potential trade, and quite often they are filled to capacity, sometimes even more, to maximize their profits.

Here you can see a Matatu fully loaded with people, with a few people even hanging onto the back of the vehicle

Occasionally, you may come across some unroadworthy vehicles on the road, such as this Land Rover. It is clear that the chassis is visibly bent but the vehicle is still travelling in a forwards direction. This vehicle should not be on the road, but unfortunately is still being used.

Once I was returning to Nairobi from Mombasa when I happened to pass this vehicle! As you can see, this vehicle should never have been on the road. It is completely battered, with no headlights or windscreen, but the driver has the car's number plate showing in

the front, behind where the windscreen would have been. This driver thought that just because he is showing the car's number plate, it makes his car legal, so he can drive his car on the roads. Behind him is a brand new Mercedes Benz. I followed the yellow vehicle for a few miles until he veered off down a path towards his village. Vehicles such as this one or the Land Rover are not normal cases, but you do see them occasionally.

People in the rural areas also use other means of transport. For example, in northern Kenya camels are used to transport goods.

In other areas they use donkey carts.

Or oxen/bullock carts.

Or even bicycles.

You can see that this bicycle is fully laden with fresh fruit for sale, with one person in the front holding the handle and guiding the bike while the person at the back is pushing it.

When I took this photograph I was just interested in the fruit vendor, but later, when I looked at the photograph again, I saw this very tall man standing there as well. He must have been at least seven feet tall, which is amazing!

Another means of transport is the Arab Dhow. In the olden days these were used to transport spices and slaves between East Africa, the Middle East and the Far East as well.

In Mombasa, at the Kilindini Creek, a ferry is used to transport vehicles and people from Mombasa Island to the south coast.

And this is the best part – tourists in Kenya are transported in these luxury vehicles, with open windows and a sun roof too, so that everyone can stand up and take photographs.

Or for a touch of luxury the tourists can be ferried around the various parks and game reserves in private planes like these.

4. Sport

Kenya's sporting prowess and achievements are well-known around the world, so I'm not going to say too much about them here. Suffice it to say that of all the Olympic Athletics medals ever won, Kenya holds nearly 50% of them!

During the 2016 Olympics in Rio De Janeiro, Brazil the first ever inaugural Olympic Laurel was presented to Kipchoge Keino who is Kenya's finest Athlete and Olymplian having set world records and winning gold medals at the Mexico Olympliacs. This Laurel was given for his achievements in the field of Athletics and also because he is a great philanthropist. In his home town of Eldoret he has built, at his own expense, a primary and a secondary school for over 90 orphaned children where they are given free education and taught all kinds of sports.

Small as it may be in comparison to other countries, Kenya's sporting achievements belie its size, with it being world-renowned also in motor-rallying and cricket.

Motor-rallying in Kenya started in 1952 when the then British citizens organized a motor-rally to commemorate the coronation of Queen Elizabeth II. At that time it was called the East African Coronation Safari and the course crossed through all of the three East African countries, i.e. Kenya, Uganda and Tanganyika.

The East African Coronation Safari was always held during the Easter public holidays, starting on the Thursday afternoon and finishing on the Monday, after having raced day and night through all three countries. In those days there were very few tarmac roads. Most of the rally took place on roads with no tarmac, which in rainy seasons became very muddy and in dry seasons very dusty. Hence, either way, it was a very challenging rally. The most treacherous sections of the rally were in the Usambara Mountains between Moshi and Dar es Salaam in Tanganyika, as these were passed through during the night. The other treacherous section was the Meru Embu road on the eastern slopes of Mount Kenya. This was because of the black cotton soil there, which is so thick that if you got stuck in it, it was very difficult to get out by single-handed and you would need to be pulled out by a tractor or pushed out by lots of people. Erik Carlson, a famous rally driver, once escaped the mud by rolling his Saab rally car, with the help of others, during the 1963 Safari Rally.

This Meru Embu road has now been tarmacked, thanks to the financial and physical aid from the British government. It was officially opened by Prince Philip, the Duke of Edinburgh, in 1985.

View of Meru Embu road

This Coronation Safari Rally has grown in stature since then. In 1960 it was renamed the East African Safari Rally, and kept that name until 1974 when it became, simply, the Safari Rally. Then after the collapse of the East African Community in 1977, Kenya took over the control and the running of the rally and its name again changed to the Kenya Safari Rally. The KSR has since been recognised by the World Rally Championship and is now on the WRC's world circuit.

Kenya's most popular and successful Safari Rally driver ever was Joginder Singh, who was also known as the 'Flying Sikh"'or the 'Simba ya Kenya"'which means 'the Lion of Kenya'. He was the first driver to win the rally outright three times, but his most memorable win was in 1965 when he won it jointly with his brother, Jaswant Singh. This was no mean feat, as they were the first non-Europeans and the first Asians to win the rally. The other first that they achieved was that their car number and starting position were both number one, and they finishedat number one position both on the road and on points. Their car, a second-hand Volvo, was a private entry, which the two of them had prepared themselves. They beat all the works-sponsored rally teams such as Lancia, Datsun, Toyota, Subaru, Peugeot, Mercedes, Saab, Ford and Dodge.

Myself with the late, legendary Joginder Singh

Another Asian local driver from Uganda, Mr Shekhar Mehta, has been the most successful driver in the history of the event, with five outright victories, in 1973 and 1979–1982.

Kenya also has a long history of playing cricket. During its pre-independence days,

Kenya used to play test matches against Britain, India, Pakistan and South Africa. This is the type of cricket ground they used to play on.

Kenya really came onto the World Cup scene for cricket when it defeated the great West Indies team during the 1996 Cricket World Cup in Pune, India. It was like a fight between David (Kenya) and Goliath (West Indies). Since then Kenya has been playing test matches during all the World Cups.

Golf is also a very popular sport and all the major towns in Kenya have high quality, well-maintained golf courses and clubhouses too. This is all thanks to the British legacy.

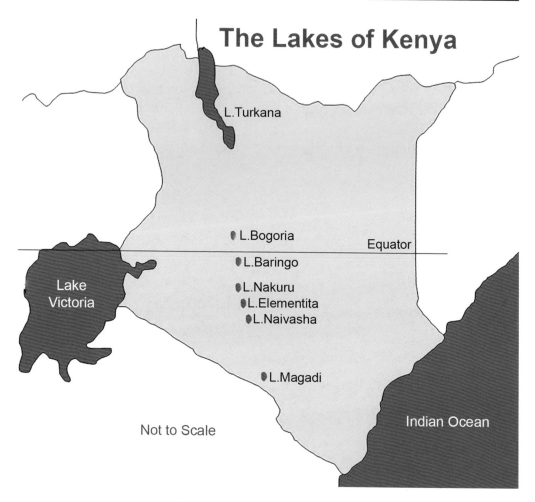

The Lakes of Kenya

L.Turkana

L.Bogoria

Equator

L.Baringo

Lake Victoria

L.Nakuru
L.Elementita
L.Naivasha

L.Magadi

Not to Scale

Indian Ocean

Kenya has several lakes, all of which are located within the Rift Valley, except for Lake Victoria, about 5% of which is in Kenya, with the rest in Uganda and Tanzania. Lake Victoria was named after Queen Victoria, who was the monarch of Britain in the early twentieth century.

The biggest lake in Kenya is Lake Turkana, formerly known as Lake Rudolf, which was named in honour of Crown Prince Rudolf of Austria. Some of these lakes are fed by the rivers that run off the Highlands and these rivers are dependent upon the rainy seasons.

In Kenya there are two rainy seasons, which essentially follow the movement of the sun. The sun is over the equator on 21st March and 21st September and the rains follow the sun. The long rains are from March through to May and the short rains are from October to November.

This is a view of Chania Falls during a dry season. Access to these falls is through the grounds of the Blue Posts Hotel in Thika, which is about 30 miles from Nairobi. You can just about see a trickle of water flowing down the left side of the falls.

Another view of Chania Falls, this time with the water at full force during a rainy season.

This photograph was taken in the Masai Mara Game Reserve. I am standing in the sun and the big blue coloured background is actually a huge wall of rain falling on the Masai Mara plains! This rain is about 50 miles away from where I'm standing!

Seen here, again in a rainy season, are the Fourteen Falls, which are located about 25 miles east of Thika town.

These are the Nyahururu Falls, found in the Aberdare Range (a mountain range north of Nairobi). Access to them is through the grounds of Nyahururu Lodge.

These falls are about 200 feet in height and were originally called Thompsons Falls, so named after the English explorer who first saw them. The nearby town was also called Thompsons Falls. Long after Kenya gained its independence from Britain, both these names were changed to Nyahururu. Nyahururu town stands at nearly 8,000 feet above sea level, making it an effective training ground for Kenyan athletes. Near to the town is a very long, steep hill called 'agony hill' which is where most of the athletes do their training.

Nyahururu Falls and curio sellers.

A tour of Kenya's lakes

This is a sunset over Lake Victoria, with people fishing. Lake Victoria is the world's second largest freshwater lake, after Lake Superior in North America. Although Kenya has the smallest portion of the lake in comparison to Uganda and Tanzania, fishing is still big business here. The town nearest to Lake Victoria is Kisumu, and this is where Kenya's Fisheries Department for the Ministry of Fisheries Development is located. The biggest fish found in the lake is the Nile Perch, which weighs about 100 pounds (about 50 kilos).

Rift Valley Lakes

Starting in the south of Kenya and travelling northwards, the first of the Rift Valley lakes you arrive at is Lake Magadi. Lake Magadi is a saline, alkaline lake approximately 100 square kilometrs in size. It is replenished mainly by the saline hot springs that are located at the northwest and south of the lake.

This lake was discovered by the early British settlers and was bought by a British firm called Imperial Chemical Industries (ICI). They started a company, the Magadi Soda Company, for which they built a factory in Magadi for the manufacture of soda ash from trona, a mineral with various industrial uses, including glass-making, which is mined from the lake. ICI also built, at the company's own expense, a tarmac road between Nairobi and the lake, a distance of about 75 miles, on which to transport the soda ash. They built a railway line from Lake Magadi to Kajiado (a town 80 kilometres south of Nairobi), and then from Kajiado to the station in Konza (a town 160 kilometres south east of Nairobi), which is on the main railway line between Nairobi and Mombasa, in order to transport the soda ash to the port in Mombasa. The factory in Magadi produces nearly 90% of the world's requirement of soda ash.

In December 2005, ICI sold the Magadi Soda Company to an Indian company called Tata India.

During the dry seasons the lake is covered with soda which after evaporation leaves behind the soda crystals.

View of the lake from near the factory site

The Lake's water surface

This is the lake's water edge. Note the different colours due to the soda's evaporation and the resulting crystals.

Lake Magadi is also well known for its wading birds, especially the flamingos.

Lake Naivasha, a freshwater lake, is the highest lake in the Rift Valley, at an altitude of about 6000 feet. It lies just north of Mount Longonot and is described as an ornithologists paradise as more than 400 varieties of birds have been spotted here. In the middle of the lake there's a crescent-shaped island called (logically) Crescent Island, and many birds nest here. Access to Crescent Island and the lake is through the Lake Naivasha Country Club. Many hippos can also be found here at the lake. The town next to the lake is aptly named Naivasha town.

The most common birds seen here are the cormorants, which build their nests in the branches of acacia trees. Their droppings are so acidic that they can kill the tree, leaving behind just a bare tree stump.

The next lake, **Lake Elementeita**—another soda lake —is located between Gilgil and Nakuru town, which in turn is on the fringes of Lake Nakuru National Park, the home of the world-famous flamingos. Lake Elementeita is not very popular as it is located off the beaten track. The small hill in the background is also known as Delamere's Nose or the Sleeping Warrior which somehow resembles the shape of Lord Delamere's Nose.

Lake Elementeita

Lake Nakuru—a freshwater lake— lies within the Lake Nakuru National Park. The road leading to it is through Nakuru town, by the Stag's Head Hotel which is an old colonial hotel.

Nakuru high street

The road to the park passes by tall acacia trees; once you come out of the trees a magnificent view awaits you, as you have your first sight of thousands of flamingos.

A typical first sighting of thousands of flamingos

A typical first sighting of thousands of flamingos

There are two types of flamingos – the Greater and the Lesser Flamingo. The Greater Flamingo is bigger in size and has mostly pink feathers while the Lesser Flamingo is smaller in size and has dull white feathers. Both varieties can be seen in these photographs.

The flamingos are unable to fly straight upwards from ground level like other birds. For them to be able to fly, they must first start running slowly while flapping their wings. As their speed increases and their wings beat faster and faster, they are able to 'take off'. In this respect they're rather like aeroplanes, only prettier!

The flamingos have a very odd-shaped curved beak. This is because of the way they feed themselves. Flamingos are grazers, 'hoovering' the lake just under its surface. In this photograph you can see them moving forward with their beaks in the water, while simultaneously sucking up and filtering their food from the water.

As the flamingos spend most of their time in the lake, they build their nests in the water but lifted out of the water and away from the water's edge. This is in order to keep the eggs safe from any predators. They usually lay just one egg at a time.

The flamingos have only two natural predators – the fish eagle and the baboon. I did, however, once see a hyena attack and catch a flamingo, as it couldn't fly away fast enough.

A ffsh eagle at Lake Nakuru

At the southern tip of Lake Nakuru is a big hill, called Hyrax Hill, which overlooks the lake. These are the views of the lake from the top of the hill.

Lake Nakuru is also the centre for breeding the endangered rhinos in Kenya. As such, when you are at Lake Nakuru you may well see rhinos, and occasionally, buffalos. Lake Nakuru isn't home to many predators. You won't see any lions or cheetahs there, although you might spot the occasional leopard.

The next lake is another freshwater lake called **Lake Bogoria,** which is located about 70 miles north of Nakuru town. It is famous for its beautiful scenery, its hot springs, its flamingos and its herd of Greater Kudus – a big antelope with curved horns, and a bluish-brown to reddish-brown coat with between 4 and 12 vertical white stripes on it.

Lake Bogoria

Views of Lake Bogoria's hot springs, taken at the same place but at different times
In 1986   *In 2011.*

As this lake is fed by several rivers and there is no obvious outlet for the water, the water level just increases. Hence this hot spring has been completely submerged under water, but it is still spitting out hot water

These are the flamingos at Lake Bogoria. They are migratory birds and they migrate between Lake Bogoria and Lake Nakuru.

If you go to Lake Nakuru and find very few flamingos there, you can rest assured that you'll find most of them at Lake Bogoria, and vice versa.

Lake Bogoria has such clean water that the water's surface looks as if it has a metallic sheen to it.

6. Nairobi

Nairobi—from a Masai word meaning 'and of cold water'—is the capital of Kenya and is situated at an altitude of about 5500 feet. It is located close to the geographical centre of Kenya and has a long history.

When the construction of the Kenya Uganda Railway line reached Nairobi, the workers stopped here, as it was nearly the halfway point between Mombasa and Kampala, the ultimate destination. The construction team started to build small shanty huts with tin roofs, in the city.

My grandfather's images of Nairobi in the early 1920s. Nairobi House clearly seen here

They then slowly started to build stone-walled buildings as well which became shops, offices and houses. Thus Nairobi soon began to expand and flourish. Over a period of one century, Nairobi has become a very modern, cosmopolitan, international city with modern communication systems and an equally developed infrastructure.

When the British were ruling Kenya, they built the infrastructure needed to run the country efficiently. A few of the most notable structures are the Parliament buildings, City Hall, the Supreme Law Courts, the sports and golf clubs, the international hotels and the main roads. When Kenya gained its independence from Britain, it took over and maintained all these structures and added more to them.

If you were to catch an overnight flight (maybe with Kenya Airways) from Britain to Nairobi, you would probably enter Kenya's northern airspace around the time the sun rises over Lake Turkana. Then, on the final landing approach to Nairobi, the plane would pass to the west of the Aberdare Mountain Range and Mount Kenya and this is the view you would have from the plane if you looked out of the left-side window. As the crow flies, Mount Kenya is about 50 miles away from the Aberdare Range.

On a clear day you can see Mount Kenya from Nairobi, from the top of Uhuru Park Hill, even though Mount Kenya is about 100 miles away. You can even clearly see the Lewis Glacier on Mount Kenya.

Sometimes, when you get up early in Nairobi you can see there's going to be a wonderful sunrise. When I had one such chance, I ran outside and this is the view I got that morning. The structure on the left is the Nyayo National Stadium, Kenya's athletics stadium.

Equally, if you go to the top of Uhuru Park Hill, you might see this wonderful sunrise over Nairobi.

Then, after seeing the sunrise as you walk down towards the Uhuru Park Lake you will be treated to these views.

Nairobi's landmark is the 28-storey Kenyatta International Conference Centre (KICC), which has a helipad on its roof and a revolving restaurant on the top floor that provides beautiful panoramic views over Nairobi. The KICC houses many Government and non-governmental offices. It also has a domed Plenary Hall, with a seating capacity for 5000 people and this is where all international conferences are held.

Next to the KICC is a statue of Mzee Jomo Kenyatta, the first President of the Republic of Kenya, who passed away peacefully in his sleep in 1979.

President Kenyatta always used to carry a fly whisk with him and this became a symbol associated with him. Hence, on this statue, the fly whisk is clearly visible in his right hand.

After the death of President Kenyatta in 1979, his Vice-President, Mr Daniel Arap Moi took over office and became the second President of Kenya.

President Moi similarly had a symbol associated with him; he used to carry a white stick with him, which in Swahili is known as a 'Rungu'. A rungu is a wooden stick with a ball head which can be used as a weapon of offence or defence.

There is a monument in central Nairobi called the Moi Monument, which is topped with the 'rungu'. This monument was built to commemorate the rule of President Moi.

The Moi Monument

Kenya achieved its independence from the British on 12th December 1963 and the whole ceremony was conducted in Uhuru Gardens. These gardens are located on Langata Road which is on the way to Nairobi National Park. In these gardens there is a monument called the Uhuru Monument which was erected to commemorate Kenya's independence.

This three-sided monument has a pillar in the centre underneath which is a statue of the White Dove of Peace on top of a pair of clasped hands signifying unity. On one side you can see people lifting up the Kenya flag – this signifies Kenya's struggle for independence. On the other side you can see a shield with two spears – this is Kenya's coat of arms.

Nairobi City Skyline

View from Uhuru Park Hill

The other important monuments and buildings in Nairobi are:

The Parliament buildings

The Supreme Law Courts

Nairobi City Hall

The McMillan Memorial Library

Lord McMillan was an American who had settled in Kenya and he owned a mountain called Ol Donyo Sabuk, which is about 40 miles from Nairobi and clearly visible from the city. The peak is only 7000 feet high (remember Nairobi is 5500 feet high). As he had no dependents, when he died he donated all of his money to build this library in Nairobi. He was then buried on Ol Donyo Sabuk.

In front of the McMillan Memorial Library there are two statues of lions. These are similar to the ones found in Trafalgar Square in London.

The Norfolk Hotel, built in 1904, is the oldest and the most luxurious hotel in Kenya. In the olden days, when the White farmers used to come into town from their farms, they would come and stay here. They would have their afternoon tea sitting on the Lord Delamere Terrace, which is the verandah at the front of the hotel. In this photograph, on the right-hand side, you can see the people sitting on the terrace

The Norfolk Hotel initially belonged to a chain of hotels owned by the Block family and called Block Hotels. It was then bought out by the Lonrho Group, still under the same name. The Fairmont Group then bought it and renamed it 'The Fairmont Norfolk Hotel', and they renovated the front of it. This is how it looks today.

The Hotel Sarova Stanley was originally The New Stanley Hotel. It is situated in the centre of Nairobi. This hotel was also used by the White farmers when they came into Nairobi. In the foyer of this hotel there are lots of old photographs of old Nairobi.

A third hotel is the Hotel Ambassadeur, which was built in 1961. Before independence, since non-whites were not allowed to stay in The Norfolk or The New Stanley Hotels, the Hotel Ambassadeur became the hub for all the leading African politicians whenever they came into Nairobi. A regular visitor to this hotel in those days was Jomo Kenyatta, who later became Kenya's first President.

Nairobi has developed and prospered, and now has many very well-regarded hotels.

The Lillian Towers

The Hilton Hotel

Within the vicinity of the Hilton Hotel there are quite a few interesting landmarks. One of these is the statue of Dedan Kimathi on Kimathi Street.

Dedan Kimathi was the leader of the Mau Mau movement which fought for Kenya's independence from the British government, who eventually caught him and put him to death. One of his assistants was Jomo Kenyatta who went on to become Kenya's first President.

About 100 meters away away from Kimathi's statue is another statue of a former Kenyan trade unionist and statesman, Mr Tom Mboya. This statue is also about 100 metrs away from the exact spot where Mr Mboya was gunned down on the streets of Nairobi, on 5th July 1969.

Next to this statue is the building of the Kenya National Archives which was previously the headquarters of the Kenya Commercial Bank.

And next to the National Archives is the Hotel Ambassadeur. Then, if you look across the road you will see Kencom House, which is now the new headquarters of the Kenya Commercial Bank.

The area between the Hilton Hotel, the National Archives, the Hotel Ambassadeur and Kencom House is the final terminus of all the buses and taxis which serve the outlying areas around the city. All the commuters come and go from here. So this area in effect is known as the center of Nairobi.

Nairobi has two more buildings of note – the Post Office Tower and Nyayo House. Both these buildings are visible from the top of Uhuru Park Hill.

The Post Office Tower

The Nyayo House

During the British rule, the British wanted to enjoy their leisure time. They built exclusive clubs for themselves in each town in Kenya. In Nairobi, there is the Nairobi Club, Royal Nairobi Golf Club, Parklands Sports Club and Muthaiga Golf Club. The Muthaiga Golf Club is located in the most affluent area of Nairobi called unsurprisingly Muthaiga. Many countries Ambassadors and High Commissioners have their residences in Muthaiga.

The Muthaiga Golf Club, nowadays, is the main venue for the Kenya Open Golf Championships and is also where some of the filming took place for the film *Out of Africa*.

The Muthaiga Golf Club

Now we all know about the American drive-in cinemas. But did you know that the first drive-in cinema outside of the United States was built in Kenya in the 1950s by Twentieth Century Fox Cinemas. It was aptly named 'The Fox Drive-In Cinema'. It has a screen 120 feet long and 70 feet high and the cinema has a capacity for 1200 vehicles. I remember the first film that I saw there, in 1958, was an Indian Bollywood movie called *Mother India*.

After the success of this drive-in cinema, Kenya built another cinema called 'The Belle Vue Drive-In Cinema' in the South 'C' area of Nairobi, which is on the road out of Nairobi towards the Jomo Kenyatta International Airport.

On Nairobi's main central road, Kenyatta Avenue, there are two very important monuments. The first one is the African War Memorial, with statues of three African soldiers.

This memorial is dedicated to all the African soldiers who fought for the British Empire during the two World Wars. The inscription on the plaque, written in three languages – English, Swahili and Urdu - reads as follows:

THIS IS TO THE MEMORY OF THE NATIVE AFRICAN TROOPS WHO FOUGHT, TO THE CARRIERS WHO WERE THE FEET AND HANDS OF THE ARMY, AND TO THE OTHER MEN WHO SERVED AND DIED FOR THEIR KING AND COUNTRY IN EASTERN AFRICA IN THE GREAT WAR, 1914 – 1918. IF YOU FiGHT FOR YOUR COUNTRY, EVEN IF YOU DIE, YOUR SONS WILL REMEMBER YOUR NAME.

The other memorial on this road, next to the Post Office Tower, is the Galton Fenzi Memorial, which was erected in 1939. This memorial is now protected by steel railings to prevent it from being vandalised.

Mr Galton Fenzi pioneered many of the road routes in Eastern and Southern Africa and these are inscribed on the memorial. He was the first man to drive from Nairobi to Mombasa, which he did in January 1926 in a Riley. He pioneered the Nairobi to Dar es Salaam to Malawi and the Nairobi to Khartoum routes.

The Nairobi Millary Stone, which is fitted onto the Galton Fenzi Memorial, has the latitude, longitude and altitude of Nairobi in exact figures.

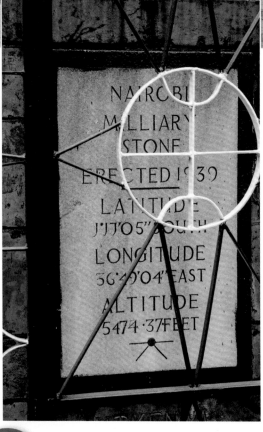

Very close to both the Galton Fenzi Memorial and the Post Office Tower is the Nairobi Municipal Market. This was the one and only market in Nairobi in pre-independence times.

In those days you could buy all your fresh vegetables, fresh meat and all sorts of fish from here. Within the dome of this market there is painted a very big Coca-Cola sign. They also used to be a painted dunlop tyres sign since been painted over. This sign has been there for decades and certainly since I first started going to the market as a very young child when my father had a shop there. So I can say, hand-on-heart, that this sign is more than 55 years old.

1985   2011

This market still sells flowers, fruit, vegetables, meat and fish but is no longer a major market. Instead it essentially serves the tourist market and you can buy all sorts of souvenirs, wooden carvings, oil paintings, batiks and curios.

In Nairobi and throughout Kenya, huge shopping malls have now been built, which cater for everyone and for all tastes.

Nairobi's two main shopping malls are the Sarit Centre and the Westgate, both of which are in the Westlands area of the city.

The Sarit Centre

The Westgate Centre

Views of the Sarit Centre

Views of the Westgate Centre

In the Westgate shopping mall, on certain days, they hold a Masai Market, where you can buy all sorts of Masai souvenirs.

One of Nairobi's famous landmarks was Nairobi House which was built around the 1920s. It was situated at the junction of Government Road (now Moi Avenue) and Lord Delamere Avenue (now Kenyatta Avenue). It functioned as offices until the 1980s when its ownership changed hands.

Nairobi House in the 1920s

Nairobi House in 1986

This is how the buildings and the road on the right of Nairobi House looked in 1986.

View of Moi Avenue in 1986

All the buildings on this part of Moi Avenue are now listed buildings.

Then, about five years ago, a fire destroyed Nairobi House. This is how the spot looks now, with the listed buildings obscured by trees which have been planted there.

One of Kenya's most important institutions of higher learning is the University of Nairobi, which is Kenya's largest university and is located close to the Fairmont Norfolk Hotel.

This university started its life in 1956 as the Gandhi Memorial Institute. Then on 28th June 1963, the then President of Tanganyika, Mwalimu Julius Nyerere, re-opened this Institute as a university. Its name was changed to the University of East Africa, serving students from Kenya, Uganda and Tanganyika. Its coat of arms is sculpted in stone on the front of the university building. It bears the symbols of the three countries – Kenya's lion, Tanganyika's giraffe and Uganda's crested crane. There is also a book, symbolising knowledge and three sets of flames on rods, which symbolise the light of knowledge.

A point to note about this sculpture is that if you look very closely at the bottom right corner, you'll see that it was created in 1962 by somebody called F. V. FOIT.

After the break-up of the East African Community in 1968, the University of East Africa was split into three independent universities: Makerere University in Uganda, the University of Dar es Salaam in Tanzania, and the University of Nairobi in Kenya. The University of Nairobi to this day still has the Gandhi Memorial Library with a statue of Mahatma Gandhi there.

In front of the library is the Great Courtyard, used previously for graduation ceremonies, and to the left of it is the Fountain of Knowledge, known as the Professor Yagnik Fountain.

The Professor Yagnik Fountain

The Great Courtyard

Nairobi National Museum

The Nairobi National Museum was originally called the Coryndon Museum, in honour of Sir Robert Coryndon, a former governor of Kenya. After Kenya gained its independence, the Coryndon Museum changed its name (in 1964) to the National Museum of Kenya.

Here at the National Museum, you can see the statue of 'Ahmed' the elephant, the only animal in the world ever to have been protected by a presidential decree. 'Ahmed' was also known as 'the King of Marsabit National Park' because he possessed enormous tusks, weighing 67 kilos each. In 1970 President Kenyatta passed a decree to protect him and thereafter he had a 24-hour armed guard. He died a peaceful, natural death in 1974 and his body has been preserved and is now on show at the National Museum.

On the subject of elephants, on the outskirts of Nairobi, and just within the boundaries of the Nairobi National Park, is the Daphne Sheldrick Elephant Orphanage. This orphanage, for both orphaned elephant calves and baby rhinos from all over Kenya, was founded and is still managed by Daphne Sheldrick, the widow of one of Kenya's best known game wardens, David Sheldrick.

Because these calves are orphans, the keepers become their surrogate 'mothers'. They look after them 24 hours a day. They even sleep with them, feeding them special milk every three to four hours. The calves follow the keepers all the time, sometimes even holding onto their arms with their trunks.

On the outskirts of Nairobi, in the Langata area, there's a giraffe rescue centre which has been set up as a breeding centre for the endangered Rothschild Giraffe. This giraffe is differentiated from other reticulated giraffes by having an extra horn on its forehead.

Also in the Langata area is the Karen Blixen Museum.

Karen Blixen was a Danish lady who settled in the Karen suburb of Nairobi. In fact, the Karen suburb is named after her. While in Kenya she lived in a house called 'Bogani' and she also owned a coffee estate. After divorcing her husband, she met an English big- game hunter, Finch Hatton, with whom she formed a relationship. After his tragic death in an aeroplane crash, she sold her coffee estate and moved back to Denmark.

Blixen was also an author and she is best known for her book *Out of Africa* which is her account of living in Kenya. This book was subsequently made into a Hollywood film which has already been mentioned. The costumes and clothes that were worn by Robert Redford and Meryl Streep during the filming are on display in the museum, which was originally Blixen's house. The museum gives an insight into Blixen's life.

Eating out

One of the best places to eat a good meal with a variety of meat in Nairobi is The Carnivore restaurant on Langata Road, next to Wilson Airport. As you can see from the menu, on the day the photograph was taken you could choose from camel, crocodile and ostrich meat amongst others. The food is served to you at your table and the waiters constantly keep bringing more food to you.

Nairobi being such a cosmopolitan city, you also get many other varieties of food in restaurants, e.g. pure vegetarian, Indian, Chinese, Thai, Japanese and African foods

In addition to these high-end foods, you can also buy good food items from the street vendors like this sugarcane seller. In his handcart he has sugarcane sticks and he will cut a small length, about two feet long. He will then put a plastic bag on one of his hands and with a knife in the other will skin and cut the sugarcane into small pieces which you

then chew on. This is an experience worth having and it will not upset your stomach as it's just pure sugar and handled very hygienically.

In the same way, you can also eat pineapple slices from the street vendors.

Religion

Kenya is fundamentally a Christian country but all other religions are well tolerated, and their places for worship are as follows:

Muslims – the Jamia Masjid – 1985

Muslims – the Jamia Masjid – 2011

Ismailis - the Ismalia Mosque

Hindus - the Swami Narayan Temple

Sikhs - symbol of Sikhism

In Nairobi, about 200 metrs from the Parliament buildings, is the Baden–Powell house. In 1907 Lord Baden-Powell founded the Scout movement, which spread world-wide. He died in 1944 and this building was constructed in his memory. The foundation stone for it was laid by the then Governor of Kenya, Sir Evelyn Baring. The money for this building was donated by the people of Kenya, the Scouts themselves, and the Round Tablers of Kenya. Lord Baden-Powell's wife, Olivia Baden-Powell, was the founder in 1910 of the Girl Guides movement. The two of them spent the final years of their lives in Kenya, at the Outspan Hotel in Nyeri, staying in one of the lodges known as Paxtu Lodge, which is now a museum.

Lord Baden-Powell created the Scouts' Motto – 'Be Prepared'.

He also created the Scouts' Promise:

> On my honour, I promise that I will do my best,
> To do my duty to God and my country,
> To help other people at all times
> And to obey the Scouts' Law.

Lord Baden-Powell died in 1944 while Lady Baden-Powell died in 1977. Since they both had made Kenya their home, it's only fitting that they be buried there. Their joint grave is in Nyeri cemetery. On their tombstone there's the Scouts' sign for 'gone home'. Their grave is seen here.

Finally, I'd like to share this photograph, taken around 1964 or 1965, when I shook hands with Lady Baden-Powell. She had come to perform the opening ceremony of the Jubilee Cabin at the Scout's Rowallan Camp in Nairobi. Some Senior Scouts had formed a Guard of Honour for her and I am on the extreme right of the photo. Lady Baden-Powell shook hands with everybody who formed the Guard of Honour.

THROUGH THE LENS

-Powell inspects Scouts

When the World Chief Guide, Lady Baden-Powell, arrived at Nairobi Rowallan Camp on Saturday to erform the official opening ceremony of the rebuilt Jubilee Cabin, a guard of honour of Senior couts was drawn up to greet her. Our picture shows Lady Baden-Powell, who is accompanied by he Assistant Area Commissioner of Senior Scouts, Mr. Edward Heathcote, shaking hands with Senior ea Scout Nigel Bramich as she made the inspection. After opening the Cabin, presentations of the

On the south-west of Nairobi are a group of hills called the Ngong Hills. These hills are visible from the outskirts of Nairobi.

Then on some clear evening, you might be able to see a beautiful sunset like this, behind the Ngong Hills.

The Ngong Hills from Nairobi

7. Western Kenya

To get to Western Kenya, you should start your journey from Nairobi. Since it is the capital and geographical heart of Kenya, Nairobi's transport infrastructure most efficiently facilitates travel to the rest of the country. Your route would go either from Nairobi to Limuru and then on to Naivasha, or from Nairobi to Kikuyu, through the Rift Valley and on to Naivasha. From Naivasha the route would then go through Nakuru, Timboroa and Kericho, before finally reaching Kisumu.

If you were to take the Limuru route, you would travel along the top right side of the Rift Valley, giving you this view of Mount Longonot.

The more scenic route, however, is via Kikuyu, because you travel down the Rift Valley Escarpment and can stop at various points to view the great expanse of the Rift Valley and wonder at what nature has created for us humans.

As you drive along this road, maybe take a moment to consider that when the railway line from Mombasa to Kampala was being built, this is the terrain the team were dealing with and imagine the challenges they faced.

- At the bottom of the Rift Valley at a place called Kedong Valley, you pass a Catholic Church which was built by the Italian prisoners of war during the Second World War.

Then you start the gentle ascent towards Mount Longonot. After about two or three miles you come to a junction. The road left goes to Narok town and eventually to the Masai Mara Game Reserve, while straight on goes to Nakuru. From here you're able to see Mount Suswa on your left-hand side.

You then pass both Mount Longonot and Lake Naivasha on your left and drive through Naivasha and Gilgil towns and pass Lake Elementeita before reaching Nakuru town, which is only 100 miles from Nairobi.

From Nakuru town you take the Nakuru–Eldoret road and after thirty miles you reach Timboroa town

and turn left on to the Kisumu road. You're now in the Highlands area of Kenya, which is a very rich agricultural land and it's no wonder it was called the White Highlands of Kenya. Here you will see huge plantations of wheat, barley and maize and then tea when you approach Kericho town. Kericho town and its suburbs have flourished because of the tea plantations.

Tea plantations

A close-up view of tea plants

Kericho has one very famous hotel called the Tea Hotel Kericho. It was built during the colonial era and still stands very proud today. As you enter the hotel, you can see the opulence of the colonial era. This hotel is worth visiting, even if just to have afternoon tea and cakes and to explore its grounds and buildings.

In Kericho town there is a huge Sikh Gurdwara (Sikh place of worship). There was a Sikh man, Sant Baba Puran Singh Ji, who used to run an engineering workshop in the town. He was a very devoted religious man and founded a Gurdwara and became the founder Saint of the Guru Nanak Nishkam Sewak Jatha. In this Gurdwara you're able to see and read about his way of life while he was living in Kericho.

Continue on from Kericho, and after about 70 miles you reach Kisumu town. Kisumu is the third largest city in Kenya, the administrative headquarters of Western Kenya and a port city on Lake Victoria. It also has an international airport.

Kisumu skyline viewed from Lake Victoria

Attractions in the town include the town clock, the Kisumu Museum, an impala sanctuary, a bird sanctuary and Hippo Point. Despite its name, Hippo Point is better known as a viewing point for the unobstructed views it offers of stunning sunsets over the lake than for its occasional views of hippos.

Kisumu city clock

Kisumu high street

The US President Barack Obama's father is from the village of Nyang'oma Kogelo, which is 37 miles from Kisumu on the Kisumu–Busia road.

On the same road, you cross the equator. This equator sign, erected by the Lions Club of Kisumu, is the best equator sign in the whole of Kenya because all the other equator signs just have the word 'Equator' painted on a single metal sheet and fitted across two metal upright poles while this one is a huge three dimensional

That's me by the equator sign on the Kisumu-Busia road

As the equator passes through Kenya and divides Kenya into two halves, there are various places where the equator crosses the roads.

The following photos show the equator signs on Kenya's roads.

On the Meru-Embu road

On the Nanyuki-Nyeri road

On the Nanyuki-Nyahururu road

On the Nyahururu-Nakuru road

On the Nakuru-Lake Bogoria road

On the Nakuru-Eldoret road

One interesting feature of the equator is the way the water swirls in the northern and southern hemispheres.

In the northern hemisphere the water swirls in a clockwise direction whilst in the southern hemisphere it swirls in an anti-clockwise direction. Whilst if you were standing directly on top of the equator line there is NO swirling of the water, it just flows down in a straight line. This is known as the CORIOLIS effect and you can actually see this effect on my website at www.fotolandimaging.com.

So with this simple experiment you can very accurately chart the course of the invisible equator line!!! How amazing is this?

8. Coast

Travel to Kenya's coast from Nairobi, a distance of 300 miles or 500 kilometers, involves three options – air, rail or road.

By air, unsurprisingly, is the quickest and involves an hour's flight to Mombasa from Nairobi's Jomo Kenyatta International Airport (JKIA).

By rail, it takes about thirteen hours on an overnight train to Mombasa from Nairobi. On this train the First Class cabins have sleeping and dining facilities. Second Class cabins have only sleeping facilities, while Third Class cabins have only benches to sit on with no sleeping facilities. Travel on this train and you may well feel nostalgia for how the early settlers in Kenya used to travel. This is a narrow-gauge train and as such is a slow train. This train leaves Nairobi at about 18:00 hours and reaches Mombasa at 07:00 hours the next morning. You are likely, along the way, to have been treated to a very good sunset and sunrise, although obviously these are weather dependent. You may have also been able to see Mount Kilimanjaro.

The final travel option is by road. The journey can be done in four hours if there is need for speed or it can take a whole day, perhaps involving stops for photographs and picnic along the way. Just for information – Nairobi is at an altitude of 5474 feet and as such the journey involves a substantial, albeit gradual, descent to sea level passing through various vegetation and climatic zones.

Make an early morning start from Nairobi, leaving behind the city crowds and passing residential and industrial areas and the JKIA. The dual carriageway then gives way to single carriageway all the way to Mombasa. You pass the Athi Plains about 30 miles outside Nairobi and enter the Machakos Plains and sometimes see sights like this.

These furrows in the road are caused by the tropical sun's very strong rays combined with the weight and movement of heavy transporter truck tyres. In places, these furrows can be more than six inches in depth and as such small vehicles especially have to drive carefully to avoid them.

Once past the Machakos Plains you enter the Sultan Hamud Hills, about 70 miles from Nairobi. It is then a continual, noticeable descent until you come out of the hills. On a clear day, Mount Kilimanjaro is visible from here.

About 100 miles from Nairobi there is a very nice resting place called Hunter's Lodge. Snacks and meals are available here together with overnight accommodation.

A further 10 miles down the road, at a town called Makindu, is a very prominent Sikh temple called the Makindu Sikh Gurdwara.

This Gurdwara was constructed in the wilderness because many years ago some people claimed to have seen Guru Gobind Singh (the founder of Sikhism) riding on his white horse there. When this news reached Nairobi, the Sikhs started to visit Makindu to worship the place where Guru Gobind Singh had been 'seen' and as a result this town grew bigger and bigger. Nowadays, this Gurdwara in Makindu is a very important religious institution in that it caters for people of all races and religions and is also a convenient rest stop for travellers to and from Mombasa. It offers a huge dining facility which provides free food 'LANGAR' 24 hours a day. There are even rooms with beds, several with attached bathrooms, for stays for up to two nights, both for worshippers and other visitors. There is no charge to use these facilities, but most people donate money to the Gurdwara for its upkeep.

There is a hospital across the road from the Gurdwara, known as the Makindu Hospital although its official full name is 'MATA VEERAN KAUR AMRIT HOSPITAL'.. Veeran Kaur Amrit was the mother of Harbans Singh Amrit, a prominent architect from Nairobi, and he built this hospital in her memory. (MATA is a Punjabi word and means 'mother').

For the next 40 miles up to Mtito Andei, which is the halfway point between Nairobi and Mombasa, the landscape changes to open plains with lots of baobab trees.

Baobab fruit

Legend has it that many centuries ago this land suffered a long drought and all the animals were dying of starvation. The baobab trees still had lots of fruit growing on them, so God asked these trees to give their fruit to the starving animals, but the trees refused to do so. God got so angry that he plucked them out of the ground by their roots and pushed them back into the ground upside down. That is why you now see baobab trees with thick trunks and small branches which look like roots growing out of them. This is the reason why the tree is also known as the 'upside down tree'.

The baobab fruit has a green velvety skin and is about six to eight inches long. It is used in traditional African recipes and also to make juice.

Mtito Andei, the next town and half way to Mombasa, is a good resting point for meals and accommodation. Also to be found here is the entrance to the Tsavo West National Park, from the Kilaguni Gate. The road into the park leads first to the Kilaguni Lodge and then to other attractions in the park, e.g. the Mazima Springs and the lava flows. All of the 'Big Five' animals, i.e. lion, elephant, buffalo, rhino and leopard, can be found in this National Park. In addition, oryx (an antelope with two sharp horns and grey-coloured skin) can be found in the vicinity of Mazima Springs.

A buffalo herd at the Kilaguni Lodge watering hole.

Tsavo National Park is the biggest National Park in Kenya. It extends from Mtito Andei to Voi, a distance of 50 miles. It's divided into the Tsavo East and Tsavo West National Parks by the main road and the railway line that pass through it. Just by driving down the main road you may, if you're lucky, see herds of elephants and small antelopes. On this road, besides all the small game, I have seen huge herds of elephants and Greater Kudu and once I've even been chased by a rhino.

If you were to take a detour via Kilaguni Lodge, you would rejoin the main Mombasa road about 30 miles down, at a place called the Man-Eaters Lodge, named after the 'Man Eaters of Tsavo'. They were made famous during the building of the Kenya Uganda Railway line, as the man-eaters (lions) were found in this Tsavo National Park.

Between Voi and Mombasa both the road and altitude keep descending – you can clearly see this in this photograph.

With 40 miles left to reach Mombasa, at Mackinnon Road you come to a mosque, which has in it the tomb of Sayeed Baghali Shah Pir Padre. He was a very religious Muslim man who died in 1902 during the building of the railway line.

The road approaching Mombasa is so heavily used that it has been badly degraded. There are lots of potholes and the surface is very uneven.

However, after having braved bad roads and seen some wildlife, you now start feeling the heat and humidity of the coast as you finally reach Mombasa.

Mombasa is the second-largest city in Kenya, with a population of over one million people, and is situated on the east coast of Kenya. It has a prominent port and an international airport. Mombasa's proximity to the Indian Ocean made it a historical trading centre.

Mombasa as an island is separated from the mainland by two creeks – Tudor Creek in the north and Kilindini Harbour Creek in the south. It is connected to the north mainland by the Nyali Bridge, to the south mainland by the Likoni Ferry and to the north-west by the Makupa Causeway, alongside which runs the Kenya Uganda Railway line. The port serves Kenya and other landlocked countries, e,g. Uganda, Zaire, Rwanda, Burundi, Congo and South Sudan by linking them to the Indian Ocean.

Mombasa has many important landmarks, one of which is the two pairs of elephant tusks made of steel that are located on Moi Avenue, formerly Kilindini Avenue.

The tusks were built by British engineers in 1952 to commemorate the coronation of Queen Elizabeth II.

The other important landmark is Fort Jesus, which is situated near Mombasa's Old Town.

In the sixteenth century, the Portuguese were exploring and colonising various regions of the world. When they arrived in Kenya, they found that Mombasa Island was a natural harbour and conquered it. To protect Mombasa from foreign invaders, mainly the Arabs, the Portuguese, under the orders of King Philip I of Portugal in 1593, built a fortress which they named Fort Jesus. For the next three centuries Fort Jesus was won and lost nine times by various nations who wanted control of Mombasa.

When the British colonised Kenya in the early twentieth century, they used it as a prison until 1958, after which they converted it into a historical monument and museum.

Then, in 2011, UNESCO declared it a World Heritage Site because it is one of the most outstanding and well-preserved examples of a sixteenth-century Portuguese military fortification.

Close to Fort Jesus is a scaled-up model of an Arab coffee/tea urn.

At the base of it is a place to hold hot burning charcoals which keeps the tea or coffee hot and at the same time the drink becomes a very strong brew. The vendor also carries small drinking cups with him which he keeps on clicking together to draw attention to himself. He will then serve you the tea or coffee in these cups. You will need a good stomach to drink this strong brew.

Fort Jesus now is a very popular destination for both local and foreign tourists. It is located to the east of Mombasa Island, adjacent to Tudor Creek, which leads to the Old Port of Mombasa where all the dhows come and go.

This is one of the dhows in full sail in Tudor Creek. These dhows do not have engines, and only use their cloth sails to steer their course. They are dependent upon the wind and its direction. They sail in the Indian Ocean by following the monsoon winds. These dhows were initially trading dhows: the Arabs would take slaves from Mombasa and the surrounding areas to the Middle East and India. When the monsoon winds changed direction, the dhows would return laden with spices.

Mombasa's Old Town, which has all its Arab and Portuguese architecture still well preserved and clearly visible, is next to Fort Jesus and the entrance to the Old Town is next to Ali's Curio Market.

There are many narrow roads with buildings overhanging them. Below are some photographs of Mombasa Old Town.

Another important landmark of Mombasa is its ex-colonial hotel, called the Castle Royal Hotel. It is white in colour and located on Moi Avenue. From the exterior you can see its opulence and grandiose architecture.

A further important landmark is Mombasa's retail market, called the Mombasa Municipal Market. It was formerly known as the Mackinnon Road Market as the road in front of it is called Mackinnon Road. Here you can buy varieties of fruit, vegetables, meat and spices and if something's not immediately available the market traders will source it for you.

I think this market was built around 1914, because in the market there's a pillar on the base of which there's an inscription from a British firm based in Bristol, called John Lysaght Ltd.

Mombasa Municipal Market

From Wikipedia I got the following information "The Company **John Lysaght,** founded in 1857, was an iron and steel company based in the United Kingdom, established in Bristol with facilities in Teesside. The company was acquired by GKN in 1920 and it became defunct in 1921."

As mentioned earlier, Mombasa is connected to the north by the Nyali Bridge, to the south by the Likoni Ferry and to the mainland by the Makupa Causeway.

In this photograph, you can see the new Nyali Bridge in the background and the old Nyali Bridge in the foreground. The Old Nyali Bridge was a British-built pontoon bridge, meaning that it would move up and down with the movement of the tides. It was a single carriageway bridge so vehicles could only pass in one direction, with guards on either end controlling the flow of traffic.

This bridge served Mombasa and the north coast until the 1980s when the Japanese government made and donated the new Nyali Bridge. When the new bridge was built the old pontoon bridge was finally demolished and is no longer there. This photograph was taken just two weeks before its demolition.

The Likoni Ferry connects the mainland to the south coast and Kilindini Creek leads to Kenya's international harbour and port and also to the headquarters of the Kenya Navy.

As you approach the entrance through which to board the Likoni Ferry from the Mombasa town side, you come across a huge baobab tree, the base of which, I think, is more than 15 feet in diameter.

And near here you also come across street vendors who sell fresh coconut fruit and cassava chips. The coconut is cut and peeled in front of you for you to then drink its sweet juice. When the juice is finished, the vendor makes a spoon out of the coconut husk and scoops the pulp from the inside to give you. This pulp is delicious!

The cassava vendor will cut and fry the chips right in front of you and will then sprinkle some salt and red chillies on them before giving them to you to eat. This also tastes fantastic. Both are completely fresh and prepared cleanly and hygienically in front of your eyes.

The coconut seller

The cassava fryer

Coconut fruit on the tree

Breakfast!

Barbecue dinner by the swimming pool

The whole of Kenya's coastline has white sandy beaches, with an abundance of sunshine. Hence it becomes a playground for many sports.

White sandy beach

You can go deep-sea fishing

Or go on jet-skis

Or go wind-surfing

Or go on camel rides

Or if you feel lazy, you can just relax by the beach on a sun lounger

There are lots of hawkers and vendors on the beach who want to sell you their art pieces, batiks, oil paintings, wooden carvings, or sometimes even seashells, even though the collection and sale of seashells is strictly prohibited.

The best beaches in Mombasa are in two areas to the north, called Nyali and Bamburi. Here you'll also find the best hotels, e.g. the Nyali Beach Hotel, Bamburi Beach Hotel, Whitesands Hotel, and quite a few more. Access to the beach is restricted as it is through these hotels. The only beach with unrestricted access is the Bamburi Beach.

In the vicinity of Bamburi is a wildlife conservation area called the Bamburi Nature Trail, where you can see hippos and huge tortoises. This conservation area is an old disused quarry and the land has been reclaimed to make it into a conservation area.

There is also a crocodile farm nearby where you can go and see the crocodiles in all stages of growth. At the same time you can have a meal there and taste the crocodile meat. The crocodile meat, in my opinion, tastes just like fish and is very tasty.

If you were to travel north towards Malindi, which is about 75 miles from Mombasa, you would pass Nyali and Bamburi beaches and then cross the Mvita Bridge. Nearby is a snake park with many varieties of snake.

About 20 miles further on, you come to a place called Kikambala which has a lovely hotel called the Sun 'N' Sand Hotel.

Sun 'n' Sand hotel, Kikambala

Up until the early 1990s the only way to go to Kilifi, Malindi and Lamu was by a ferry across the Kilifi Creek. The getting-on and getting-off points are visible in the centre of this photo.

On 15th May 1991 President Mwai Kibaki opened the Kilifi bridge over the Kilifi Creek. It was built by the Japanese Government and opened up the northern coast of Kenya.

The Kilifi Bridge

After a further 20 miles from Kikambala you arrive at Kilifi and cross Kilifi Creek via the new Kilifi Bridge, and eventually you reach a historical site called the Gedi ruins, about 10 miles outside Malindi. These ruins are of an old Swahili town and feature a mosque and stone houses. It is now a National Monument.

After the Gedi ruins you enter Malindi, which is a very popular tourist area because of the good hotels, good food, white sandy beaches, plentiful sunshine and good social life. Malindi has a small domestic airport. In the late fifteenth century, the Portuguese explorer Vasco da Gama visited Malindi and erected a pillar which bears his name and which still stands to this day.

Vasco da Gama pillar – front and rear views

Near Mombasa, on the south coast, after passing the Likoni Ferry, there is one game reserve which is not very well known, called the Shimba Hills Game Reserve. This reserve is the only place in Kenya where you can see the Roan and Sable Antelopes. Roan Antelopes are so named for their roan colour, which is reddish brown, whilst Sable Antelopes are darker black rather than dark brown. It is worthwhile visiting this reserve just to see these beautiful antelopes.

9. Mount Kenya

Mount Kenya is the highest mountain in Kenya and the second-highest mountain in Africa after Mount Kilimanjaro. The highest peaks of the mountain are Batian at 17,057 feet (5,199 metres) and Nelion at 17,021 feet (5,188 metres), both rock-climbing peaks and Point Lenana at 16,355 feet (4,985 metres), which is frequently used by tourists for hiking.

Mount Kenya is a free-standing extinct volcano, situated close to the centre of Kenya and straddling the equator. In fact, the equator line passes through its centre, making it a unique mountain, in that it is the only place in the world where you find permanent snow and ice on the equator. Kenya derives its name from Mount Kenya.

The mountain has several vegetation bands from its base to the summit. It starts off as very rich agricultural land, followed by thick forest with huge quantities of bamboo in it. The forest ends at around 11,000 feet, giving way to alpine vegetation. Many alpine species are endemic to Mount Kenya, such as giant groundsels, lobelias and seneccios. With such diverse vegetation and an abundance of wildlife as well, Mount Kenya was declared a National Park, and in 1997 it was listed as a UNESCO World Heritage Site.

A local tribe, the Kikuyus, live around the base of Mount Kenya, and they believe that their God, 'NGAI', and his wife 'Mumbi' live high up on the mountain. As such, this mountain is worshipped by them. Locally, this mountain is also known as 'MILIMA KIRINYAGA' (means Mount Kirinyaga). There have been several cases when local people, without proper clothing, footwear or protective gear have been found climbimg the mountain. Once a local Kikuyu man was rescued from the slopes of Batian. He had no gear, ropes or shoes and when rescued he said he was just trying to reach his Ngai!

Mount Kenya has three popular trekking routes. The 'NAROMORO ROUTE' from the south-west side of the mountain, starting from Naromoro town, is the shortest, easiest and quickest route up and down the mountain. The 'SIRIMON ROUTE' starting from Nanyuki and Timau towns, west of the mountain, goes up the Mackinders Valley and reaches the Mackinders Hut. The 'CHOGORIA ROUTE' starting from Chogoria town, goes up from the eastern side of the mountain.

The route I'm going to describe is the Naromoro Route, as it's the most popular route, and starts from the Mount Kenya National Park gate, shown in the photograph.

This gate is at about 7000 feet above sea level. During the dry weather season, an SUV can be taken up to 10,000 feet, at which point there is a meteorological station for all the weather readings. There are also a few huts for overnight accommodation. The mountain rescue team of the National Park is also based here.

But during the wet season you have to start walking from the gate. To cover the 3000 feet up to the meteorological station can take a full day. This is good for acclimatisation, as you are walking very slowly and have little chance of developing mountain or altitude sickness. It is quite a picturesque track, up and over rivers and small valleys. Over one of these valleys, some British engineers built a bridge called Percival Bridge, in memory of Lt D.H. Percival who was killed in 1961 whilst climbing in Aden.

On the bridge they stuck a sign: Maximum load 10 tons. Elephants requested to cross in single file.

This is the end of the road at the meteorological station and the trek starts from here. The barrier is only opened during mountain rescues when an SUV is needed to go higher from here.

The meteorological station is constructed in the middle of the bamboo forest and occasionally all kinds of animals just wander through like these Sykes monkeys.

After an hour's walk through the forest from the meteorological station, you suddenly come out of the bamboo forest into the alpine vegetation and the start of the 'vertical' bog. This bog or wetland during the rainy season is very hard to get through as all the time you are plodding and splashing through mud and water. This can be very taxing on the legs. After another hour's walk you come to The Cave, which can be used as an emergency shelter. By now the steepest part of the day's walk has been accomplished. All this time you are walking along the right wall of the Teleki Valley, which is the main valley on the mountain. Then after a further hour's walk you start descending into the Teleki Valley and the giant groundsels, lobellias and seneccio plants start coming into view.

You keep descending into the valley in a diagonal direction until you cross the Teleki River via a small wooden bridge.

After crossing the river you start ascending to the Naromoro Lodge Hut. This hut is at about 13,000 feet. So to cover the 3,000 feet from the meteorological station to the Naromoro Lodge Hut has taken you a whole day.

Naromoro Lodge Hut with Mount Kenya's peaks

In the vicinity of this lodge are some small rodent-like creatures. They're called Rock Hyrax and are considered to be the nearest relative of the elephant!

This is because the shape of their feet is the same as an elephant's and also by the way their intestines are coiled inside their bodies, making them the closest relative of the huge elephant.

On a clear evening you will have your first glimpse of all Mount Kenya's major peaks - Batian, Nelion, Point Lenana, Point John and also Arthur's Seat. The Lewis and Diamond glaciers are also clearly visible.

The next day with an early morning start you trek all the way to the head of Teleki Valley, and then turn right to climb the scree - which is a steep slope covered with loose stones and pebbles. It's very difficult to go up in a straight line as every step you take tends to involve slipping back half a step, making it a painstaking task. But this problem is easily solved by diagonally traversing the scree. This method is less tiring on the muscles, and makes the climb less arduous.

This is a view of the scree. You can see the gradient of the slope. That huge rock in the background is Point John, with Batian partly obscured by the clouds.

About halfway up the scree you're able to see Mount Kenya's biggest glacier, the Lewis Glacier. This glacier extends all the way up to the top of Point Lenana – the tourist peak, and our final goal.

Lewis Glacier in January 1968

Lewis Glacier in August 2005

Point Lenana in January 1968

Point Lenana in August 2005

These four photos clearly demonstrate the effect of global warming on the environment; more than half of the Lewis Glacier has disappeared in the last 47 years.

At the bottom end of the Lewis Glacier is Lewis Tarn, which receives all the water from the melting glacier. Lewis Tarn is also the starting point of the Teleki River in the Teleki Valley.

It takes about two to three hours to climb up the scree. The best thing here is that it only takes about half an hour to run down the scree, using a method called 'scree running'. Scree running involves running downhill by taking long steps and jumps. As you land from each jump you should land on the heel of your boot and make sure that you're leaning backwards. This way you are in control of your own speed going down.

After the scree is finished you then turn left climbing towards Point Lenana and upon rounding a corner you get your first view of the Austrian Hut and the Porters Shelter at an altitude of about 14,700 feet.

The Austrian Hut is so named because the Austrian government funded its construction. In September 1970 an

Austrian doctor, Dr Hans Judamier, fell and broke his leg while descending from Batian. His companion came down the mountain and raised the alarm. The Kenya Mountain Rescue team, of which I was a member, were fortunately all 'caving' at Mt Suswa at that time. When we got the call for the rescue we immediately left for Mt Kenya. We got to Mackinders Hut (base for the final climb to Batian) in two days. On the third day, 9th September 1970, Captain Jim Hastings, a helicopter pilot, was bringing us supplies when a sudden strong gust of wind blew his helicopter out of control and he crashed onto the rocks. Sadly the accident was fatal.

The Austrian Hut

129

Unfortunately the Kenya Mountain Rescue team were unable to rescue Dr Judamier because we were only volunteers and inadequately trained. However the Austrian government, upon reading of his plight, sent their own Mountain Rescue specialist team and they rescued him. In appreciation of the efforts of the Kenya Mountain Rescue team, the Austrian Government built this hut to replace the original 'Top Hut' which had burnt down.

View of the crashed helicopter

HERE ON
9th SEPTEMBER 1970
CAPTAIN JIM HASTINGS
GAVE HIS LIFE
HELPING TO SAVE OTHERS

Memorial plaque for Captain Jim Hastings

Above is the photo of Point Lenana with the Porters shelter on the right and the Top Hut on the left.

Below is the photo of the burnt out Top Hut with the Porters shelter still intact as it was a few metres away from the Top Hut and thus was saved from the fire.

This is the view of an early morning sunrise over Nelion, taken from the former Top Hut site.

At this site, you have about 600 feet to go to the summit of Point Lenana. As you climb, if you look back this is the view you have of the Teleki Valley, with the Naromoro Lodge Hut just a small speck in the valley and you realise just how high you have climbed and what an enormous mountain this is.

All the time you are climbing, Nelion peak is always visible to your left, obscuring Batian.

As you climb towards Point Lenana's summit, you scramble over huge rocks which are interspersed with ice from the Lewis Glacier.

Top of Point Lenana

After a final push, reaching the top of Point Lenana brings a sense of the achievement of having climbed the second highest mountain in Africa. From the top you have magnificent views over the northern and eastern side of the mountain. The northern side looks towards Isiolo town while the eastern side looks towards Chogoria.

This is me on top of Point Lenana with Nelion in the background. Although I have climbed Point Lenana 23 times, this is the only photo of me at the top of it.

This is the most common view of Mt Kenya taken from the southern side, i.e. Nairobi, Thika and Sagana side.

But not many people have seen Mt Kenya from its opposite northern side. This is how it looks like from the Timau side.

10. The Rift Valley

To see the full expanse of the Great Rift Valley, you need to travel about 25 miles north-west of Nairobi to arrive at a viewing point at an altitude of 8000 feet which overlooks the Rift Valley.

From this viewpoint, you can see the small farm holdings in the foreground, while in the background is a free-standing extinct volcano, Mount Longonot. Also in the background you can see the Aberdare Mountain and Mua Hills Ranges, which form the western wall of the Rift Valley. Beyond that, the land drops down towards Kisumu, Lake Victoria and eventually to Uganda.

To the left of Mount Longonot is Mount Suswa (not visible in this photo), which has many caves that I believe, though I am not a caver myself, are very good for caving and are used by people who participate in caving.

Two views of Mt longonot from different angles. The first is from the Rift Valley view point and the second from Lake Naivasha. The distance between the points where these two photographs were taken is about 40 miles.

If you travel from Nairobi to Naivasha by road, via Kikuyu and through the Rift Valley, besides enjoying fascinating views, at the bottom of the Rift Valley at a place called Kedong Valley, you will find a small Catholic church which was built in 1942 by some Italian prisoners of war during the Second World War.

These prisoners of war were captured in Abyssinia—present-day Ethiopia—and brought to Nanyuki at the foothills of Mount Kenya. Then, in 1943, three prisoners of war escaped from their camp and climbed Mount Kenya. After climbing they returned to their camp. After the war, one of the prisoners, Felice Benuzzi wrote about his exploits in a book entitled *No Picnic on Mount Kenya.*

Kenya, being such a stable country in Eastern Africa, received a lot of foreign aid in the 1960s and 1970s. Part of this aid involved telecommunications infrastructure. On the floor of the Rift Valley, at an altitude of about 7000 feet, a transmitting station was built, called Mount Margaret Transmitting Station. It has two satellite dishes, one pointing to the satellites over the Indian Ocean and the other to the satellites over the Atlantic Ocean. These two dishes enable Kenya to be in contact with the rest of the world at the press of a button.

Mount Margaret Transmitting Station with Mount Longonot in the background

Bust of Lord Baden-Powell

Lord and Lady Baden-Powell, the founders of the world-wide Boy Scout and Girl Guide movements, spent the last years of their lives in Kenya, primarily in Nyeri at the Outspan Hotel and living at Paxtu Lodge.

While staying at Paxtu Lodge, Lord Baden-Powell built a bird bath plus a table and two chairs for himself. These are still in use at Paxtu Lodge.

He also designed the Clock Tower for Nyeri Township, the design of which is shown here with the finished clock tower in Nyeri.

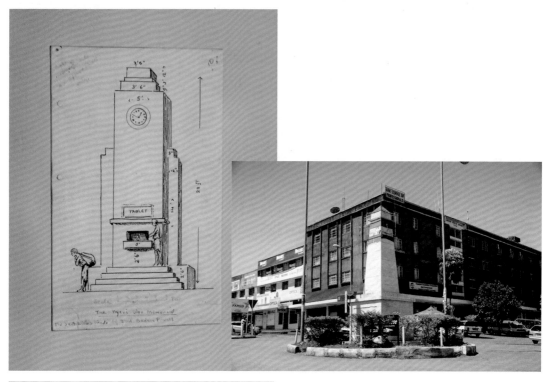

Before he died, Lord Baden-Powell wrote a final message to all the scouts which is preserved here.

The Kenya Government has now made their grave into a historical garden called the 'Baden-Powell Historical Garden'.

Kenya is also famous for two other structures found in the Rift Valley. One is the famous Treetops Lodge in the Aberdare National Park, where in 1952 Princess Elizabeth (now Queen Elizabeth II) stayed a night. On that night her father, King George VI, died in his sleep, and Princess Elizabeth inherited the throne. There is a famous saying: "Here at the Treetops Queen Elizabeth II went up as a Princess and came down as a Queen."

Another famous lodge in the Aberdare National Park is 'The Ark'. As you can see, it is built in the shape of the mythical Noah's Ark.

On a clear morning, from the viewing platform of 'The Ark', Mount Kenya can be clearly seen in the distance.

One of Kenya's most famous early settlers and pioneers was Lord Delamere. He purchased a lot of land between Naivasha and Gilgil, in the Rift Valley, where he carried out dairy, wheat and beef farming on his farm, the Soyasambu Ranch.

This is a very rare sculpture of Lord Delamere. It was originally erected in the centre of Nairobi outside The New Stanley Hotel in the road named Lord Delamere Avenue, which after Kenya's Independence was renamed as Kenyatta Avenue.

11. Mount Kilimanjaro

Although Mount Kilimanjaro is not within Kenya, it is still worth mentioning, because all of the photographs you see of it with wild animals in the foreground are from the Kenya side, taken from the Amboseli National Park, which is at its base.

View of Mount Kilimanjaro from the Machakos Plains

Mount Kilimanjaro from Amboseli National Park

This is the view of the summit of Mount Kilimanjaro as seen from the aeroplane when flying from Nairobi to Mombasa.

And this is Uhuru Peak, which is the HIGHEST point in Africa, i.e. top of Mount Kilimanjaro.

12. Wildlife

Before I start telling you about the big game wildlife, let me firstly tell you about the other birds and animals which play their part in the African wildlife kingdom.

First of all there is a beautiful and elegant bird, the crested crane, or as it is more commonly known, the crown bird.

This crested crane is the national symbol of Uganda and is depicted on its coat of arms. Crested cranes are always found in pairs as they stay together for life. They have a beautiful plumage that glows in the sunlight. They make a very characteristic sound when they are flying, which once you've heard you won't ever forget.

Then there is the ostrich, which is the world's tallest flightless bird and it lays the world's biggest egg. An adult ostrich can grow as tall as 9 feet in height.

As you may be aware, in the bird kingdom it is generally the male bird that is prettier and more brightly coloured than the female bird, so that he can attract a mate. In the ostrich the female is a dull brown colour, while the male has a very black plumage, with the exposed skin on its neck and legs normally grey coloured. But during the mating season, the male's skin colour changes to a deep pink, again to attract the females.

After mating, the female ostrich can lay between 20 and 40 eggs. The male and female will then take turns to incubate the eggs and to turn the eggs over while counting them to make sure none have been taken by predators. They will very furiously defend their nest and eggs from any predators, e.g. hyenas, baboons, vultures and snakes especially the python.

The male African weaver bird is very brightly coloured with bright yellow feathers. During the mating season, he will lovingly and laboriously build a nest for his mate. As you can see from this photograph, he's just started to build the nest, using green grasses and twigs.

He starts building the nest *Half way done* *Nearly finished*

While he's building the nest, his female companion keeps a very keen eye on him, making sure he makes a good job of it!

The other males in the flock are similarly building nests to lure the female weaver towards them. So on one acacia tree you can see lots of nests.

Once the male has built the nest, he will invite his female companion to come and inspect it. She has a very sharp eye for detail, and will painstakingly check it out. If the nest meets with her approval, she will stay in and the male will join her. But if she does not like the nest, for whatever reason, she will break it and throw it to the ground, as is seen in this photograph.

Once the nest has been destroyed, the male has to start all over again to build another one. In the meantime, one point to note is that after the female has destroyed the nest, she'll go and examine the other males' nests and if there is one she approves of, she'll enter that one, mate with that male and lay her eggs while the first male weaver loses out.

Besides these elegant birds, there are also the carrion-eating birds, e.g. the vultures and the marabou storks. On any kill the vultures are the first birds to arrive on the scene. After the meat-eaters have had their fill and gone away, the vultures will then devour any meat left behind.

Once the vultures have cleaned the carcass, the marabou storks then play their part.

I would describe these marabou storks as 'flying disposal factories'. These birds can swallow whole chunks of bone which their stomach acids will then dissolve.

In this photo you can see that this stork is just about to swallow whole a huge piece of bone. Once the bone has been swallowed the stork then flies off to her nest to digest it.

After the 'flying disposal factory', we also have a 'land disposal factory', in the shape of the hyena.

If a hyena gets to the kill before the vultures and storks, he'll eat everything, including the bones. With his very strong and powerful jaw muscles the hyena breaks the bones and then eats them. When a hyena is finished with a kill there will be nothing left there and thus nature creates a way to ensure that all creatures involved in the food chain get their share of it. There have been reports that a hungry hyena will even eat human shoes as they are made of leather.

One of the greatest wildlife spectacles in the world happens on Kenya's doorstep, i.e. the great wildebeest migration.

Wildebeest crossing the Mara River in Kenya

During August and September every year, the wildebeest migrate from Serengeti National Park in Tanzania to the Masai Mara Game Reserve in Kenya. The Masai Mara Game Reserve is actually the northern tip of the Serengeti National Park. The wildebeest migrate to Kenya because of the lush vegetation and also to give birth to their young ones here. The initial migration is of small herds in long straight lines. The smaller herds then join up with other smaller herds until they form a huge herd which then becomes a marching army and then the whole horizon becomes full of wildebeest.

The herds then congregate near the Mara River and eventually they start moving down towards the river.

And here you can see them crossing the Mara River. Fortunately for them, at this time there were no crocodiles in this stretch of the river, so they were able to cross safely.

Once across river the wildebeests' migration ends and soon after they start to give birth to their young ones.

Although we are concentrating here on the Masai Mara Reserve, the wildebeest are also found all over Kenya,

e.g. in Nairobi National Park, with a sunset and the Ngong Hills in the background,

or in Amboseli National Park, with Mount Kilimanjaro in the background.

There are three types of giraffes. The most commonly seen ones are the Masai Giraffe which can be seen over most of Kenya. They are distinguished from the others by their irregular brown patches and irregular white lines.

The next one is the Reticulated Giraffe. They have very distinct brown patches with very distinct white lines. They are generally found in northern Kenya, especially in the Samburu Game Reserve.

The next one is the Rothschild Giraffe. They look like the Reticulated Giraffe but have an extra horn on their forehead.

Masai giraffe

Reticulated giraffe

Rothschild Ggraffe

Giraffes have a very unusual courtship method, involving 'necking' gently with each other. However, if two males are fighting for territory or over a female, they then fight using their necks, hitting each other very hard and making a muffled sound with the soft tissues in the necks. The fight stops only when one of them gives up or is defeated by the other.

One of the pretty looking antelopes is the waterbuck. As its name suggests it is found in the vicinity of water. This pair of waterbucks was photographed in the Lake Nakuru National Park. As you can see the male has two horns while the female has none, and they both are mid-brown in colour.

One of the most unusual antelopes I have seen is the topi. The first time I saw this topi I didn't know what the animal was, as he had a brown skin, very unusual grey markings and two small stumpy horns. Upon doing some research, I found that the topi is an antelope and is only found in the Serengeti National Park and the Masai Mara Game Reserve. The topi is also called 'the sentinel antelope', because while the whole herd feeds, one of them will always stand guard and keep a lookout for any predators.

One of the antelopes that are being bred to be domesticated is the eland. An eland stands nearly six feet tall at the shoulders and is a very sturdy animal, with light brown skin, and both the male and female have horns. This particular eland must have been involved in a territory fight and lost his horn. Having been pushed out from the herd, he was roaming on his own. Now, unless he joins up with other solitary elands, the chances of his survival are slim as he will not be able to run very fast brcause of the dangling horn.

In the Nairobi National Park orphanage there used to be a chimpanzee called Sebastian. He spent his time in his cage and became used to begging for food and cigarettes from the public. When a lit cigarette was thrown to him, he would pick it up and start smoking just like a human being does.

Chimpanzees have also been known to use a wet twig as a tool to push into an ant hill. When the twig is pulled out, the ants are stuck on the twig and are then eaten.

A six feet tall ant hill

Hippos are normally found in lakes, rivers and even springs where the water is deep enough for them to fully submerge. One thing to note here is that if hippos have any babies with them, then please do not get close to them as they will attack you. In fact this is true of all wild animals.

At Lake Naivasha

At Mara River in the Masai Mara Reserve

At Mazima Springs in the Tsavo West National Park

I took this photograph of this hippo from a hide at water level. As you can see we have eye contact with each other. She had a baby next to her, so I quickly left the hide as she could have attacked me. A hippo has two 10-to-12 inch long lower incisors, which are used very effectively both for offence and defence. I have heard that with one bite from a hippo it can cut a crocodile in two.

I was once in Nairobi National Park with my family. My son was driving my SUV and I was standing with my head out of the roof hatch, when suddenly I saw this huge 10 feet long snake, a python.

I jumped out of my SUV and started to photograph the python. For your information, a python is not poisonous. It only kills its prey by constricting and then swallowing it whole. As such, I knew I was not in any danger from this python, while the snake was more interested in searching for a place to go and hide.

When it saw my SUV it decided to climb onto it. When I couldn't find the snake I got worried as I didn't want it getting into the car where my family were. However, on opening the vehicle's bonnet, I found the python curled on top of the engine.

Upon hearing the commotion, he curled himself tighter to protect his head.

My son and daughter were sitting on the roof of the SUV while the snake was on top of the car engine. I tried to remove the snake with my hands, but he squeezed himself further into a small corner of the engine. I then had to drive 30 miles to the National Park gate to find a snake tong to grab his neck and pull him out. A snake tong is a metal rod, 25 to 40 inches long, with an alligator type of opening on one end and a handle on the other. Once the handle is pressed, it closes the alligator opening and thus the snake can be safely caught by its neck and then restrained.

Here you can see how long this python was as I'm standing on my SUV and holding the snake by its head while somebody else is holding its tail.

I then got a sisal bag, put the snake inside it and drove the 30 miles back to the exact spot where I found him and then released him. He immediately regurgitated his stomach contents, the remains of a rabbit. This explained why the python had been searching for a safe place to hide; he just wanted to finish his meal. After all this, he quietly slithered away.

An adventure worth doing is a hot air balloon ride in the Masai Mara Game Reserve. You take off just before sunrise and, while airborne, you see a beautiful sunrise as well as lots of animals beneath you. Then after about an hour's flight, you land somewhere in the reserve and are served an outdoors champagne breakfast.

So that's a little bit about the 'other' wildlife, so to speak. Now let's take a tour of the 'Big Five'.

Kenya has quite a few National Parks and Game Reserves, and the most popular ones are shown in this map.

Popular National Parks & Game Reserves of Kenya

Kenya's most popular National Parks and Game Reserves, in no specific order, are:

1. Nairobi National Park – located on the outskirts of Nairobi
2. Amboseli National Park – located 100 miles south of Nairobi
3. Tsavo National Park – located 150 miles south-east of Nairobi
4. Mount Kenya National Park – located 100 miles north of Nairobi
5. Samburu Game Reserve – located 180 miles north of Nairobi
6. Masai Mara Game Reserve – located 150 miles west of Nairobi
7. Lake Nakuru National Park – located 100 miles north-west of Nairobi
8. Lake Bogoria Game Reserve – located 70 miles north of Nakuru

When tourists visit Kenya, all they generally want to see are the 'Big Five' which are described as the most dangerous animals in Africa and these are:

1.   Buffalos
2.   Elephants
3.   Lions
4.   Rhinos
5.   Leopards

But before we even start to talk about these animals, we need to consider the issues affecting them, primarily their survival or conservation.

If we say

YES to conservation – we will have continuity of all wildlife.

But if we say

NO to conservation – we will have extinction and loss of wildlife.

So on this basis, we have to think about the inheritance that we will leave to our children.

Our Inheritance?

'The Wildlife'

Our duty is to protect, preserve and save the present wildlife for the rest of mankind, so that our future grandchildren, and their grandchildren, and their grandchildren too, may have a chance to see living wildlife and not just museum pieces!

According to my experience of travelling in Kenya, the frequency of sightings of the 'Big Five', in descending order, are as follows:

Buffalos	100%	Most abundant
Elephants	80%	Quite commonly seen
Lions	50%	Have to look for them
Rhinos	20%	Nearing extinction because of their precious horns
Leopards	1%	Very difficult to find

The buffalo is the most abundant animal, while the leopard is the most difficult animal to find.

All of the 'Big Five' can be found in all of the National Parks and Game Reserves of Kenya, the exception being the elephant who is not found in the Nairobi, Lake Nakuru and Lake Bogoria National Parks.

BUFFALO

Buffalo—Swahili name is 'NYATI'—live in big herds which give them protection from predators. There have been cases of buffalos chasing and killing lions.

One male buffalo can have a herd of 50 to 100 females as his own group. The other males will try to depose him to gain control of the females and that is why you can see this male has lost part of his horn, as he has fought successfully to retain control of his females.

As with all animals, when a male offspring reaches adulthood, he is pushed out from the herd. These males then form their own group, and are constantly on the look out for other females, at which point one will challenge the leader of the herd. Whoever wins becomes or remains the leader of the herd.

With the buffalo, once a male has been kicked out of the herd he becomes very frustrated – known as a rogue buffalo. A rogue buffalo will attack anything at the slightest provocation. Here you can see this rogue buffalo 'eyeing' me ready to attack. If I had been out of my vehicle I am sure he would have charged me and believe me, for his size he has quite a lot of speed, much faster than a human being which he can maintain over long distances as well.

The buffalos have two big curved horns with a flat base and a strong skull, enabling them to lift and throw their enemy into the air. And when it lands, the buffalo will then stamp on it and gore it with its horns!

In Lake Nakuru National Park, though, where there are no predators except the leopard, these buffalo can be seen lying down peacefully.

Buffalo are constantly covered with ticks and fleas, so to minimise them on their bodies, they will have mud baths and come out fully covered with mud. This kills the ticks and fleas, giving some temporary respite until the cycle repeats itself.

ELEPHANT

Elephant – Swahili name is 'TEMBO'.

Here is a rare chance to see elephants mating.

In this herd, the young female was in heat and the male wanted to mount her, but the female had other ideas and started running away. The male, though, who was much bigger and faster than the female, eventually caught up with her and as soon as he placed his trunk on her back she stopped running. The male then mounted her.

While this was going on, the female matriarch of the herd kept the rest of herd together at a safe distance.

When the African elephant has a young one with her and she gets disturbed or feels threatened she will charge you. Even an adult rogue male will similarly attack you if you encroach on his territory. Here an adult male is charging me. I only managed to get these two shots and then I was off to a safe distance.

In the 1970s there was an elephant in Kenya's Marsabit National Park with very huge tusks, estimated to weigh more than 100 pounds (50 kilos) each. In those days poaching was very rampant in Kenya, so Kenya's then President, Mzee Jomo Kenyatta, passed a decree to protect him. Ahmed was, and is, the only animal in the world that has ever had presidential protection. He had 24-hour armed guards to protect him. He was also referred to as the 'King of Marsabit'. He died a peaceful, natural death in 1974 at an estimated age of 55 years. After his death, his tusks were found to weigh 148 pounds (67 kilos) each, and his body has been preserved and is on display at the Nairobi National Museum.

In 1986   *In 2011*

These two photographs, taken 25 years apart, show the effect of the harsh African sun – notice how it's discoloured the statue.

This little animal, the hyrax, is described as being the elephant's closest relative!

This, allegedly, is because the shape of his feet closely resemble those of an elephant and the way his intestines are coiled inside him is similar to how an elephant's are! Bizarre indeed!

In the 1970s and 1980s there was very heavy poaching going on in Kenya. This is how a poached elephant ends its life. The poachers have killed this male bull elephant and hacked off his tusks and two of his feet. The feet are used to make footstools.

This photograph was taken in Amboseli National Park, I think a few days after this elephant was killed, as the bloodstains are still visible on the ground and not many vultures or hyenas have got to him.

Kenya eventually officially banned hunting in the country, but Kenya's two neighbouring countries, Uganda and Tanzania, did not follow suit. In the 1980s, you could still go to Tanzania and buy any quantity of ivory.

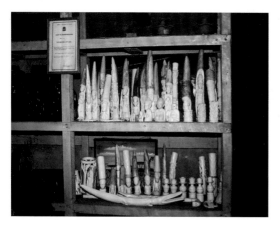

These photos of my family were taken in 1986 in a shop in Moshi, Tanzania where they were openly selling ivory and products made from ivory. The products were figure-heads in various shapes and sizes, candle holders, bangles, full tusks with figures carved in them, crocodile models and even finger rings. Now, looking at the size of the tusks and ivory products, you can imagine how many very young elephants had been killed. What a shame and what a waste of precious life.

In 1989 Kenya's then Director of Wildlife Services, Dr Richard Leaky, made a decision to burn all the ivory that had been impounded from the poachers. The main reason for this was to ban all trade, worldwide, in ivory, in the hope of saving the elephants from extinction.

Kenya had over 5 tonnes of ivory, and all of it was burnt in July 1989 in Nairobi National Park.

That is me at the first ivory burning in Kenya

Then, in the following two years, Kenya burnt all of its remaining ivory stock together with all rhino horns, cheetah, leopard and crocodile skins and all skins from other animals, including all taxidermy items from people's houses.

A stuffed lion skin which was also burnt

By burning these items, Kenya made a stand to save and protect its wildlife, for the rest of the world to follow.

Later on, the Kenya government built a monument at the first ivory burning site.

This monument depicts a dying male elephant being helped on to its feet by two other male elephants. Legend has it that a dying elephant is helped to its feet and supported by other elephants until it reaches its dying ground, where it can die peacefully.

LION

Lion– Swahili name is 'SIMBA'.

He is described as the Lord of the Jungle and it is not difficult to imagine why he is called the Lord. He is at the top of the food chain and has no natural predators; his only predator is man and his gun. His huge size, huge paws and enormous strength give him dominance over many other animals. He is truly a majestic animal.

This picture shows a lion sitting on top of an earth mound, with 'arms' crossed (like a Lord), gazing into the distance searching for his prey.

As a male lion gets older, wiser and stronger, his mane changes from fawn to black. This mane earns him pride of place in his pride of females.

But before he reaches that stage, he is pushed out of the pride when he becomes an adult. This lion is looking at me, maybe thinking his dinner is ready-made for him. If, at this stage, I was out of my vehicle, he could have very easily jumped on me. For this reason, it is very strongly recommended that you stay in your vehicle at all times while visiting any National Parks or Game Reserves in any part of the world!

Lion prides are mainly made up of female lions and their cubs. In a pride you can easily have up to ten females with lots of cubs.

If you get too close to a lion pride, a female will stare you right in the eye, and if you do not back off she will pounce on you, primarily to protect her cubs. In these two photographs you can see the lionesses are looking directly at me and telling me to back off. I gave these lionesses the space they were asking for and hence I've lived to tell the tale.

In all of these lion prides, the male lion is always lurking nearby to protect his pride from other prowling males. But he is also a supremely selfish and lazy male. He does not do any hunting himself but leaves it to the female lions. And when the female lions have made a kill, he quickly rushes forward, pushes all the females and cubs aside and has his fill of the best parts of the kill. Only when he is finished will he let the others come and have their share.

Female lions generally give birth to 3 to 5 cubs and sometimes some might not survive. I saw this female lion strolling with only one cub.

The lion is the only cat which cannot climb trees. Only at Lake Manyara National Park in Tanzania do you get to see tree-climbing lions.

Because lions cannot climb trees, when you see them trying to climb trees they look very clumsy. Here you can see some lion cubs trying to climb a tree stump while the mother lion watches.

They had a difficult time and even the one who got to the top could not come down; he stumbled and fell to the ground. The cub in the right-hand photograph is looking at me as though saying "Help – please get me down!"

When you visit the National Parks, this is the kind of SUV you would normally travel in. Everybody has a window seat, and even the roof hatch opens up to allow for a better photo opportunity.

Whenever you see a male and female lion together you know that they are in their mating season.

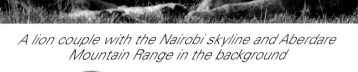

A lion couple with the Nairobi skyline and Aberdare Mountain Range in the background

During the mating season the male and female will mate for about 3 to 5 days, with mating taking place every half hour or so.

While they are mating, they do not have any need for food. So other animals, e.g. the zebras in this photograph, know that they are safe from the lions and will even stop and watch their antics.

RHINO

Rhino – Swahili name is 'KIFARU'.

One of Kenya's most famous rhions back in the 1960s was called 'GERTIE' and she lived in Amboseli National Park. She was famous because she had a huge horn. This huge horn was to be her downfall because the poachers killed her for her horn. This is a statue of Gertie and her baby which is erected at the Kenya Wildlife Services Headquarters which itself is next to the entrance to the Nairobi National Park.

In 1975 I took this photograph of this rhino in Amboseli National Park with his huge horn. In the background you can see two elephants with huge tusks too. I believe the poaching in Kenya started after 1975, which is why I was still able to take this photograph.

Rhinos are solitary animals. They defend themselves against predators by using their horn as a weapon.

As you know, the rhino has two horns, with the front one always bigger than the back one.

However, in the Masai Mara Game Reserve, I once came across a rhino who had a back horn BIGGER than the front one. This is a very rare sight as I have never seen or heard of any such rhino.

Even more rare is this photograph of the pair just as a hot air balloon was floating by.

The mother rhino will look after her cub for four years or until it becomes an adult and nearly equal to her in size. Then and only then will she let the baby go on its own. This photograph is of a mother and her baby with the Nairobi skyline in the background.

This photograph and the following one of a sunset were taken in Nairobi National Park. The sunset is behind the Ngong Hills, which are situated south-west of Nairobi and are clearly visible from the city.

LEOPARD

Leopard – Swahili name is 'CHUI'.

This is my one and only photo of a leopard. During all my travels in Kenya I have only once seen a leopard – I suppose because the leopard is the most elusive of all the cats

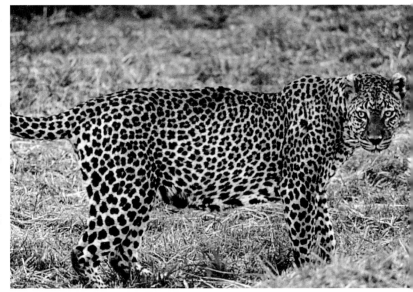

CHEETAH

Cheetah – Swahili name is 'DUMA'.

The cheetah is not part of the Big Five but it is important to talk about the cheetah as she is a member of the cat family and is more commonly seen than the leopard or the lion. Here a mother cheetah is teaching her two cubs the ways of the wild by making hissing sounds and the cubs are following her.

This is my prize photo

When the mother cheetah makes a kill, she will let her cubs eat first. Here the mother has killed an impala and is letting her cub take the first bite. You can see her sitting in the background.

In the next photograph though, she is on the kill herself. When I was taking this photograph I saw her through my telephoto lens looking directly at me and she was ready to pounce on me. The moment I saw this I ducked back into my SUV, otherwise I'm sure I would not be here now. As I have said before, respect the animals and give them all the space they need, and you will live to tell the tale.

These are a few photographs of a cheetah scouring the landscape for her next meal.

A cheetah cub

Kenya achieved independence from British rule on 12th December 1963. Thus Kenya became 50 years old in December 2013. To celebrate this milestone Kenya created a logo for it: 'PAMOJA TWASONGA MBELE' which translated from Swahili means 'TOGETHER WE MOVE FORWARD', a very strong unifying message for all the Kenyans to follow.

Kenya as a young independent country has moved forward over these past 50 years at an astonishing pace and has achieved a great deal during those years.

Kenya's independence was celebrated with a lot of pomp and pageantry. There were lots of pageants in Nairobi and lots of buildings were decorated with flags and buntings.

Kenyatta Avenue   *Kenya Law Courts*

December 1963   *December 2013*

In December 1963 the Independence celebrations were conducted at Uhuru Gardens on Langata Road whilst in December 2013 the celebrations were conducted at the Kasarani Sports Centre on Thika Road.

This year the buntings and decorations in Nairobi were few but still quite colourful.

In June 1964 President Jomo Kenyatta planted a fig tree at Uhuru Gardens on the spot where the British flag was brought down and Kenya's national flag was first hoisted. The tree has flourished well over the years and has grown accordingly.

This fig Ttee or mugumo tree (*Ficus thonningii*) is known to live for many years, making it a good symbol to commemorate such an event. It bears fruit even in the dry season thus providing food for the birds and animals.

In December 2013, President Uhuru Kenyatta planted an olive tree (*Olea africana*) here.

At Independence time Kenya only had two cement manufacturing factories namely Bamburi Cement Factory and Athi River Cement Factory. Kenya at the moment is enjoying a prosperity boom and hence many new buildings are being built all over Kenya. To keep up with this high demand for cement Kenya now has got three more cement factories, namely Rhino Cement Factory, Simba Cement Factory and Mombasa Cement Factory.

Some of the new buildings are shown below:

Building on the Nairobi to Mombasa road

Building under construction on the Outer Ring Road towards Thika

With Kenya's increasing population and the increased prosperity, the number of vehicles in Kenya has risen thereby causing congestion on the roads within the Nairobi and the surrounding areas. The rise of vehicles is owing to the number of heavy haulage trucks which transport goods from Mombasa to the landlocked countries surrounding Kenya, i.e. Uganda, South Sudan, Rwanda and Burundi. To overcome this congestion problem, Kenya is building two outer ring roads around Nairobi. One is the Northern Ring Road going from Embakasi Airport towards Ruiru and Limuru and the other is the Southern Ring Road going from Embakasi Airport towards Langata, Karen, Kikuyu and Limuru. From Limuru the road then goes on to Kenya's border with Uganda and then to Rwanda and Burundi.

This is the view of the Southern Ring Road being built near Langata

It has been reported in the local press that about 3000 heavy haulage trucks leave Mombasa daily to travel up-country transporting goods to various destinations. In this photo you can see a long line of stationary heavy haulage trucks on the Nairobi to Mombasa road. Travelling at 30mph it took me about 15 minutes to pass all the trucks. So this line of trucks was about 7-8 miles long! Just incredible.

Besides causing congestion on the roads, the heavy haulage trucks also damage the roads which can be very expensive to maintain. To overcome this, the Kenya Government has asked the Chinese Government to build a new standard (wide) gauge railway line from Mombasa to Nairobi and then on to Uganda. This railway line will reduce the travelling time from the present 12 hours to just 4 hours and the railway will also carry the goods containers. This in turn will reduce the number of heavy haulage trucks plying between Mombasa and Uganda. Hence less road congestion, less damage to the roads and less expense for road maintenance.

To ease the transport problem of the working population in Nairobi, the railways have built three commuter train stations around Nairobi, namely SYOKIMAU, IMARA DAIMA and MAKADARA Railway Stations. The trains from these stations transport people commuting to and from the outlying areas of Nairobi.

In Mombasa the old colonial hotel, The Oceanic Hotel, has been demolished and in its place an educational institute has been established called The Aga Khan Academy. The Academy overlooks the Kilindini Creek, the entry passage to Kilindini Harbour, which is the entry point for goods to Kenya and also for the landlocked countries surrounding Kenya.

Here you can see a ship going out of Kilindini Harbour and passing in front of The Aga Khan Academy.

Here is a fully loaded container ship, at low tide, passing through Kilindini Creek on its way to the Kilindini Harbour.

Mombasa is also undergoing a prosperity boom which is evident from these high-rise building shots taken from the highest building in Mombasa overlooking the Indian Ocean and Kilindini Creek.

Old and new buildings of Mombasa looking across Kilifi Creek

This is English Point Marina situated on the opposite side of Fort Jesus and across Kilifi Creek. It's a luxurious block of flats built to very high standards and comparable to flats in the western world, and priced accordingly.

On the coastal strip at the Sun 'N' Sand hotel, (which will be demolished eventually) five blocks of high rise flats, offices and shopping malls are being built which will be the tallest buildings on the whole of the eastern shore of Africa, from Cape to Cairo! This will be some achievement for Kenya.

A scale model of the high-rise buildings at the Sun 'N' Sand hotel

Roses are one of Kenya's biggest exports. They are mainly grown around Lake Naivasha in the Rift Valley. But on the northern side of Mt Kenya at an altitude of about 7000 feet near a town called Timau roses are being grown in greenhouses and are quite successful too.

14. And Finally

All good things must come to an end and so does this informative journey through Kenya. I will close by sharing with you a few more of Kenya's lovely sunrises and sunsets.

Sunset in Amboseli National Park, with a silhouette of an acacia tree

Sunrise over the Indian Ocean   *Sunrise over the Tsavo Plains*

Sunrise over Amboseli National Park

I hope that you've enjoyed reading this book as much as I enjoyed writing it and sharing my knowledge and memories of my beloved country of birth, which will always be with me in my heart.

Wildebeest at sunset

Now with all of the information that I have given to you about Kenya and its achievements I sincerely hope that you will view Kenya with a very positive perspective.

And so, with this final lovely sunset over the Masai Mara Plains, I would like to wish you 'kwaheri' (goodbye) and 'lala salama' (goodnight).

15. Some Common Swahili Words & Phrases

Jambo	Hello
Habari?	Any news?
Habari ngani?	How are you?
Kwaheri	Goodbye
Lala salama	Sleep well, or goodnight
Tafadhali	Please
Asante	Thanks
Asante sana	Thank you very much
Hapana	No thanks, or no thank you
Hapana Taka	No, I do not want it
Hakuna matata	No problem
Karibuni	Welcome